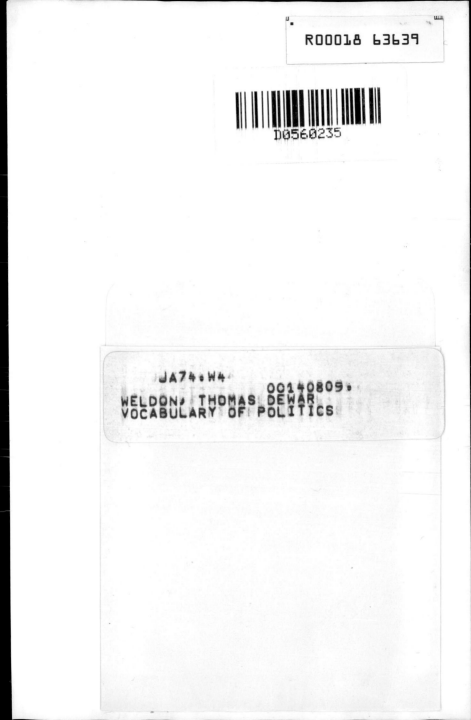

THE VOCABULARY OF POLITICS
T. D. WELDON

REPRINTS IN GOVERNMENT
AND POLITICAL SCIENCE

Editor-in-Chief: Richard H. Leach
DUKE UNIVERSITY

THE VOCABULARY OF
POLITICS

*

T. D. WELDON

PENGUIN BOOKS

Reprinted with the permission of Penguin Books Ltd

JOHNSON REPRINT CORPORATION
111 Fifth Avenue, New York, N.Y. 10003

JOHNSON REPRINT COMPANY LTD.
Berkeley Square House, London, W1X6BA

First published by Penguin Books Ltd 1953

Reprinted 1970, Johnson Reprint Corporation

Printed in the United States of America

CONTENTS

Editorial Foreword   7

CHAPTER 1: *Politics and Philosophy*   9

CHAPTER 2: *The Logic of the Classical Theories*

  1. Words and their meanings   17
  2. The illusion of real essences   20
  3. The illusion of absolute standards   30
  4. The illusion of geometrical method   33
  5. What classical political philosophy is about 36

CHAPTER 3: *The Uses of Political Words*

  1. Introduction   45
  2. 'The State'   46
  3. 'Authority'   50
  4. 'Rights'   56
  5. 'Law' and 'the Rule of Law'   61
  6. 'Freedom'   69
  7. Puzzles, Difficulties, and Problems   75

CHAPTER 4: *Political Foundations*

  1. Foundations in general   84
  2. Democratic foundations   87
  3. Hegelian foundations   101
  4. Marxist foundations   117
  5. Philosopher kings   138

CHAPTER 5: *Empirical Politics*

  1. The menace of scepticism   144
  2. Subjectivism   147
  3. Political appraisals   160
  4. Conclusion   175

CHAPTER 6: *Politics and Morals*   181

INDEX   195

Editorial Foreword

T. D. Weldon's book on political philosophy is one of a series of philosophical works which are appearing in a similar form. The series consists mainly in original studies of the work of certain outstanding philosophers, but it covers also a number of more general topics, including, besides political philosophy, ethics, logic, the theory of knowledge, and the philosophy of science.

The series is not designed to reflect the standpoint or to advance the views of any one philosophical school. Since it is addressed to an audience of non-specialists, as well as professional philosophers, the contributors to it have been asked to write in as untechnical a manner as their subjects allow, but they have not been expected to achieve simplicity at the cost of accuracy or completeness.

As its title indicates, T. D. Weldon's is a work of philosophical analysis. He is concerned not to defend, or attack, any one political system, but to exhibit the logic of the statements which characteristically figure in discourse about politics. It is of the first importance in the study of political theory, as in other branches of philosophy, to know what sorts of questions are being asked and what are the appropriate methods for finding answers to them. T. D. Weldon's book is primarily directed towards this end.

A. J. AYER

CHAPTER I

Politics and Philosophy

DURING the last century there has occurred a great change in the methods and aims of professional philosophers in this country and in the United States. To understand the nature of it and the reasons for it is difficult and perhaps impossible without a fairly thorough investigation of the technical subject matter of logic and epistemology, but at least an indication of what it is must be given at the start if the line taken in this book is to be intelligible to the non-philosophical reader. What has happened is that philosophers have become extremely self-conscious about language. They have come to realize that many of the problems which their predecessors have found insuperable arose not from anything mysterious or inexplicable in the world but from the eccentricities of the language in which we try to describe the world. Hence philosophers have largely ceased to put questions of the form 'What is truth?' and 'Do material things exist?' but ask instead 'What kind of information is conveyed by the statement that a proposition is true or that material things exist?'

The bearing of this change on political philosophy is easy to see. 'Philosophy' in ordinary language is roughly equivalent to 'attitude towards life' or even 'preference for a particular way of living'. It is common to talk of 'the political philosophy of the Russians or the British or the Americans' when what is intended is simply the type of political institutions which the Russians or the British or the Americans prefer, or are believed to prefer. Hence it comes to be supposed that the job of the professional Political Philosopher is to demonstrate that one variety of political organization is especially praiseworthy and that the others are defective. And this in the times in which we happen to live seems to amount to a demand that the political philosophy called 'democracy' should be proved correct and the political philosophy called 'communism' should be proved erroneous, or *vice versa*.

On the face of it this is quite an important undertaking. Most of us genuinely want to know what reasons there are for supporting democracy against communism or communism against democracy. We want to be sure about this because the issue is one over which a great many people have already been killed and a great many more seem likely to be in the not very remote future. It would be a disaster if that were to happen without anything substantial being achieved as a result of it.

Now although the question 'Is the political philosophy of democracy sound and that of communism unsound?' looks fairly straightforward and answerable, a little consideration shows that it is far from being clear and intelligible. To begin with, it has an unfamiliar sound. Those who have even the slightest acquaintance with the discussions of political theories which occur in standard works from Plato and Aristotle down to Rousseau and Hegel and which predominate in writers of the nineteenth and twentieth centuries outside the U.S.S.R., will realize at once that it is not a question which has always been prominent. The Greeks asked themselves whether monarchy or aristocracy or democracy was the most desirable form of government for human beings to institute; thinkers in Western Europe asked what were the proper relations of the State to the Church, and of monarchs to their parliaments; the nineteenth century was the time at which the limit of State interference with citizens was much discussed. But Democracy *versus* Communism seems to involve a different kind of question from these. Furthermore it looks like a false antithesis. The opposite to communism is capitalism, not democracy, and the opposite to democracy is dictatorship, not communism.

When these and similar points are raised it becomes clear that we are in danger of getting lost in a maze of historical enquiries and wrangles about verbal definitions. It is, therefore, tempting to avoid all this and to attempt to deal with the situation by giving up for the moment our specific question about communism and democracy in favour of a more general one about States as such. If we can say what is the right or proper relation of the State to the Individual, we can then ask whether, or how far, any set of actual institutions satisfies this condition. If it does not, then we have an adequate reason for condemning it, even though it can be proved that military, economic, and social advantages are likely to be secured by means of it. Thus we should be in possession of a sort of standard or measuring rod, which we could apply to democratic and communist institutions, or more specifically to the institutions of the U.S.A. and the U.S.S.R., and by applying this test we could say conclusively which of the two was the closer approximation to the ideal standard.

Most well-known philosophers from Plato onwards who have written on politics have accepted this as the problem with which they were concerned. They have taken for granted that 'What is the proper relation between the State and the Individual?' is a significant question to which it is both practicable and important to look for an answer, and they have also believed that they knew at least in principle the method by which an answer might be discovered. With different sets of definitions and assumptions about human psychology this is common ground to Idealist, Democratic, and Marxist theorists. I believe that all are equally mistaken, and shall devote a large part of this book to showing what is wrong with this method of approach, both in general and in the context of the competing political doctrines to which it has led.

Fundamentally, the mistake arises here, as it arose in other branches of philosophy, from carelessness over the implications of language. It arises from the primitive and generally unquestioned belief that words, and especially the words which normally occur in discussions about politics such as 'State', 'Citizen', 'Law', and 'Liberty', have intrinsic or essential meanings which it is the aim of political philosophers to discover and explain. Thus our difficulties are supposed to arise because we do not understand what the State really is. If we did know this, we should understand at once that only the Communist, or the Fascist, or the Democratic State is the genuine article, while the others are spurious imitations. Socrates, with whose enquiries Western philosophy begins, assumed that 'justice', 'courage', 'temperance', as well as 'State', were the names of things, and set himself to discover the things of which they were the names.

This mistake has led to a great deal of confusion but it was a natural one to make. Many difficulties have to be overcome before human beings can live more or less peaceably in associations and before associations can co-exist without devastating conflicts. It was, and still is, comforting to believe that these difficulties could all be overcome if only the intrinsic or essential nature of associations were properly understood. When this is accepted it is easy to proceed further and to say that enlightenment will be achieved when we discover the true meanings of the words 'State', 'authority', 'right', and the rest. To avoid apparent logical troubles it is often held that enquiry should be directed to discovering the concepts or ideas for which these words stand, but this supposed distinction between words and concepts is not important for our present purpose.

There have always been widespread doubts as to the efficacy of this essentialist assumption even in the minds of many of those who have made use of it. Beginning with the Sophist Thrasymachus, whose views on politics are reported or parodied in the first book of the *Republic*, there has been a persistent positivist opposition which has maintained that the recommended procedure of searching for the essential meaning of 'justice' and similar words is futile. It does nothing to help in the solution of any practical political problem. For this we need an accurate description of what actually happens, or tends to happen, in human associations. There is no sense in asking what ought to happen, or what would happen under imaginary ideal conditions, and disputes on such points are purely verbal and a waste of time.

This kind of view is neither so far-fetched nor so alarming as it appears to be when crudely stated by its opponents. It is incomplete rather than fundamentally wicked or mistaken. For it is true that many discussions about the meanings of political words are purely verbal, that is, they concern linguistic habits and conventions but tell us nothing about matter of fact. But it is a mistake to suppose that appraisal words such as 'good', 'ought', 'criminal', and 'wicked' have no place in our political vocabulary. As a first approximation it does no harm to say that they merely emphasize the speaker's political prejudices, but it is misleading to argue from this that his prejudices are baseless. There may be good reasons for them though the speaker himself may be unable to state these clearly and may even be ignorant of them.

The point at issue may be put thus. The gourmet who enjoys his caviar may feel pity for the schoolboy who prefers peppermint creams, but he does not condemn or blame. If he is a kindly gourmet, he may hope that the schoolboy will one day come to enjoy caviar (if he can afford to buy it). But there the matter ends. If the boy goes through life with his taste for peppermints unimpaired, there is nothing to be done about it except to say *de gustibus non est disputandum*. Now it is possible, though unplausible, to take the same line about political institutions. One can say 'Well, some people seem to like slavery or secret ballots or proportional representation. As a matter of fact, I don't; and that is all there is to be said about it'.

Probably few people would wish to maintain this position. Hence it is a good debating point for Platonists to argue that this or something like it is the only practicable

alternative to the line which they themselves recommend.
I hope to show that this disjunction between objective
standards and subjectivism in politics is a false one and that
many contemporary laments over lost political principles
are therefore quite unnecessary. There are reasons which I
find to be quite sound reasons for approving of some
political institutions and disapproving of others, but they
are not the kind of reasons which Plato and his successors
have believed to be both attainable and indispensable. It
is not my purpose here to set out those reasons in any
detail. My aim is simply to show the lines along which we
may proceed in trying to compare and evaluate different
types of political institutions and to examine both the
reliability of some political appraisals and the limitations
to which all such appraisals are subject.

I have, therefore, three objects to achieve:

1. To show that the questions put by traditional political
   philosophy are wrongly posed. In the form in which
   they normally occur they cannot be answered but can
   be shown to be unprofitable. This requires (a) some
   general criticism of the assumptions on which the
   classical political theories are based and especially of
   the nature and functions of political standards and
   ideals [Chapter 2]; (b) analysis of some of the most
   common political words, 'State', 'authority', 'law',
   and 'liberty' [Chapter 3].

2. In the light of these discussions to show that the
   theoretical foundations of political thinking which are
   claimed by Democracy, Hegelian Idealism, and
   Marxism are all equally worthless. They do not support the superstructures which they are supposed to
   support and could not conceivably do so. All of them
   alike are the result of a misconception of what needs
   to be done, since all involve the error of supposing that
   actual political institutions are imperfect copies of
   something else, that they express however imperfectly

Natural Rights, or the Idea of Reason, or the Dialectic of History [Chapter 4].

3. To show that this conclusion is in no way devastating or even alarming. It does not involve cynicism, scepticism, or the rejection of moral or political evaluations. All that is discarded is some metaphysical lumber. Indeed it is only when this is done that one can see at all clearly what are the genuine grounds of disagreement between communists and democratic politicians and give at least some indication of the way in which political appraisals are made [Chapters 5 and 6].

There are two points about this programme which require some brief preliminary comment.

In the first place my formulation of it may suggest that the writings of the classical authors on political philosophy from Plato to Lenin are valueless and not deserving of study except as historical oddities. I do not mean this. In so far as these works are concerned with verbal definitions and foundations they have indeed little of value to offer and, unfortunately, it is these sections of them which receive most attention in commentaries. On the other hand what their authors have to say in the way of description and of actual or implied recommendations is often important and illuminating. Those who want to know what Plato thought about politics would do well to study the *Laws* rather than the *Republic*.

In the second place the order of exposition I have chosen raises a difficulty as to my own use of political evaluations. For since I maintain that it is impossible to demonstrate by the application of an ideal measuring rod or similar device that one type of political institution is praiseworthy while another deserves condemnation, it may be claimed that for the time being at any rate the only way in which I am entitled to use words of praise and blame is to assert my personal preferences or prejudices. This is strictly correct.

I intend, however, to use such words in Chapters 2–4 and to use them in the ordinary way, that is, as asserting something more than likes and dislikes (at the level of caviar and peppermints). I shall not attempt to clarify or analyse this use until Chapters 5 and 6. To avoid all possibility of confusion or the suspicion that I am attempting an elaborate confidence trick, I may say at once that my political prejudices are very much the same as those of J. S. Mill and the British liberals of the nineteenth century. What is wrong with Mill is usually not his moral or political judgement but his attempt to support or fortify that judgement by means of a pseudo-scientific piece of reasoning. I do not, therefore, mind saying that some political behaviour is obviously right, or wicked, or silly. 'Obviously' is used here in the way in which it is correctly used of observations made by people with normal eyesight in a good light. In these conditions it is pointless to ask 'How do you know that this pillar-box is red?' It seems to me equally pointless to ask 'How do you know that it is wicked to torture human beings or animals?' But I think it is a mistake to use words like 'intuition' or 'self-evident' in describing such statements since these suggest that there is something odd about them which needs explanation. There is nothing odd about them at all. They are perfectly clear.

CHAPTER 2

The Logic of the Classical Theories

§1. Words and their meanings

THE title of this chapter looks a little peculiar. It may well appear high-handed or simply misleading to group together in this way a number of views which superficially at least are radically different from one another. On the face of it, Plato, Hobbes, Hegel, and Marx were in violent disagreement about something and therefore it seems unhelpful to discuss them together as if they were unanimous. It should however be remembered that the economists and the physicists who are now generally described as 'classical' also disagreed with one another substantially, yet it is easy to see why they are conveniently grouped together and contrasted with their successors in the twentieth century. The distinction in each case is one of general outlook, of what once appeared so manifest as to require no justification and to merit no enquiry; it is a matter of the unstated and often unrecognized premises from which all serious discussion takes its start.

In the case of political theories the title 'classical' is especially appropriate because the premises in question were here inherited, unchanged in all essentials, from the Greek writers of the classical period. They are not at all satisfactory and it is hard to believe that, if the Greek civilization had endured with anything like its initial vitality, they would not have been criticized and discarded. None the less they were in many ways the correct starting points for intelligent enquiry, and it was a work of genius to formulate them and to argue from them, as Plato and his immediate successors did, with such cogency as to make them both the inspiration and the prison of European thought for more than two thousand years.

I cannot do justice to them here as they involve difficult points of logic, epistemology, and scientific method, but something must be said about them in order to elucidate the method of thinking on human political associations to which they led; and it should not be forgotten that the whole intellectual development of the West, especially in scientific theorizing, has been largely dominated by these same assumptions.

The central doctrine taken for granted by all classical theorists is, as I have already mentioned, that words have meanings in the same sort of sense as that in which children have parents. Thus, if little Willie was deposited in a telephone booth at an early age, nobody may know who his parents are, but it is certain that he had parents, and it is possible to start an enquiry with a view to discovering their identity. This may well be wholly or partially unsuccessful. The evidence may be lost or the detectives may not be clever enough to discover it or to see the relevance of it. Nevertheless this is the kind of enquiry we know well enough how to conduct, and so it is reasonable to suppose that, if words and especially nouns always have meanings, we should, if we are pertinacious and fairly clever, usually be able to unearth those meanings.

But why should this supposition have been made? To answer this would require an extensive enquiry into anthropology since the supposition was by no means confined to the Greeks but was very widely spread. It is common knowledge that in the early stages of civilization names tended to have magical significance. One acquired power over a person by ferreting out his true name, earthly and heavenly names were different, Lohengrin and other heroes were forbidden to disclose their names, and the true names of gods were not to be spoken except by priests as part of a ritual. In this sort of atmosphere (and early Greek philosophy was very closely connected with religious mysticism) it is natural enough to ask for the true name of a person or a thing, and it is not difficult to reverse the order of the enquiry. One may know a name or a title, but not the person to whom it refers.

Whatever may have been the psychological origin of this type of belief, it is now clear that it was erroneous. Admittedly it was valuable as a starting point since it directed attention to the importance of language as an object of study and so gave logical analysis a beginning. It was dangerously misleading because it led insensibly to the further assumption that the analysis of words and logical forms could by itself provide information about matter of fact. Thinking by itself without any observation or consideration of instances seemed capable of finding out the true meanings of words, and this process in some indefinable way was held to give information as to the nature and relations of the things to which words referred. The application of this to political enquiries is almost painfully evident. It is that we must begin by asking for the meanings of 'justice', 'freedom', 'authority', and similar words, and that, when we have discovered what these meanings are, we shall be qualified to pronounce on whether Communism is to be praised or condemned.

The enquiry, however, is doomed to sterility because words do not have meanings in the required sense at all; they simply have uses. There is nothing divine or magical about 'justice' or 'freedom'; they are only part of the verbal apparatus we make use of for describing and criticizing certain types of human conduct. They are not the names of Ideas or archetypes of which honest transactions and fearless letters to the newspapers are more or less imperfect copies or expressions, for they are not the names of anything. To know their meaning is to know how to use them correctly, that is, in such a way as to be generally intelligible, in ordinary and technical discourse, and there is nothing more lurking behind them which you might discover if only you had some special qualifications as a member of the philosophical C.I.D. This is a very dogmatic statement. I shall do something to elucidate and to justify it in what follows, but those who rightly feel the need for further discussion must pursue the question in books on logic.

This radical misunderstanding as to the meanings of words has given rise to a whole family of philosophical illusions which make up the greater part of what is known as 'metaphysics'. Three of these are especially pervasive in discussions on politics and they must therefore be considered here. They may be called (1) the illusion of real essences, (2) the illusion of absolute standards, (3) the illusion of geometrical method.

§2. *The illusion of real essences*

The classical theory of meaning which I have outlined in the preceding section does not logically entail any particular ontology or general view of the nature and structure of the universe and its constituents. It does, however, encourage the development of such a view, and the great metaphysical thinkers of Greece, whose primary intellectual interests were mathematics, solid geometry, and astronomy, took it for granted that truths about facts could be discovered by enquiry into the meanings of words. The upshot as we find it in Plato is something like this. Anything which can be an object of knowledge must be sharply demarcated, precisely definable, and immutable. Hence it follows that perceptible objects are not as such objects of knowledge but are objects of an inferior faculty called 'opinion'. In some sense, however, perceptible things, including people, are real. Hence we must say that they somehow contain or provide instances of essential characteristics which fulfil the necessary conditions. Thus it comes to be held not merely that nouns are always the names of identifiable things, but also that the things of which they are the names are unchanging and eternal. Both views are mistaken, but both are in some ways attractive. Thus *prima facie* 'the Sun' and the names of the planets and fixed stars do have meanings which are clearly demarcated, fixed, and permanent. The names of people have the same sort of character though the people they designate are not unchanging. They grow up, grow old, and eventually die. We can get round this however by maintaining that the real or essential Socrates is eternal and does not die. Then 'Socrates' too has a fixed and immutable meaning. It designates this real or essential Socrates, the immortal soul. This is not the primary ground for the common belief in immortality, it merely illustrates the way in which primitive beliefs can be reinforced and made intellectually respectable by a mistaken theory of meaning coupled with a convenient ontology.

To turn now to the vocabulary of politics, the names of States, 'Athens', 'Sparta', and the rest are easily treated in the same way as the names of human beings. Greek States were particularly well adapted to such treatment since they were customarily personalized in popular thought by identification with tutelary gods and goddesses. And when this step was taken it was easy and natural enough to proceed further and to assume that 'courage', 'justice', 'freedom', and 'authority' also designated precisely demarcated and permanent entities of some sort, that each of them must have one single, nuclear meaning, and that it was important for us to discover that meaning. For otherwise, it could be argued, we should be unable to recognize things when we saw them (just as we might suppose we were looking at the sun when it was really the moon), and then it would be impossible for us to set about organizing States or selecting rulers with any prospect of success.

If this is agreed, the task of the philosopher in general and that of the political philosopher in particular is not difficult to formulate. It is to ascertain the true or real meanings of words, or alternatively to become acquainted with the immutable essences or Ideas for which political words stand. Precisely how he is to set about his task remains obscure. Plato himself held at one time that men are born with knowledge of these entities as part of their mental equipment and that 'philosophy' was the name of a refining or obstetric process which separated it from transient or illusory perceptions, or possibly of a special type of remembering which recovered what was once known but has been almost completely forgotten. This piece of mythology is not worth pursuing since the difficulty which it is invented to get us out of is itself a fabrication. This is evident when we observe that words and sentences are not magical incantations. They are not even natural signs which resemble or are normally associated with the things and situations which they designate. A picture of a lion may suggest courage and that of a rabbit, timidity; and it may well be the case that the historical origin of languages may be looked for in this kind of picturing. But words as we have them now are almost entirely conventional symbols, though they often inherit something from their more primitive uses.

There is nothing sacred or immutable about symbols. They are the products of human ingenuity and are as definite as we want them to be in their application. Clearly some degree of permanence and precision is demanded of them or they will not serve their purpose which is to enable us to communicate with one another, for such communication is impossible unless we can describe with some accuracy what we see and hear. But it is impossible to say that any particular degree of permanence or precision in usage is indispensable. If all language had the precision which is rightly demanded, because of their special function, in the symbols which we use in formal logic and mathematics, it would be an extremely ineffective instrument for ordinary conversation and enquiry. This fact, however, should not mislead us into supposing that since the requirements of a logical calculus are different from those of a natural language, one or both of these types of symbolic system must be somehow defective.

In the light of these general considerations it is evident that to ask 'What is the essential meaning of "justice"?' is unprofitable. Like most other words in ordinary use, 'justice' has no single nuclear meaning. There is no precise criterion for its correct employment, and it is useful largely because it lacks such precision. We can, if we find it convenient to do so, *give* it a precise or fairly precise meaning, and then it ceases to be vague or ambiguous and becomes a technical or semi-technical word. It is not uncommon, especially in legal terminology, for this to be done and for the ordinary and technical uses of a word to survive side by side as in the cases of 'fraud' and 'property'. No confusion need be caused by this because the context usually makes clear which is being employed. In such cases it is for lexicographers to decide whether to say that we have now two words, 'fraud₁' and 'fraud₂' which look and sound alike, as 'cow₁' and 'cow₂' do, or that we have one word with two different but connected uses. What is futile is to puzzle ourselves as to whether the American or the Russian use of 'democracy' is the true or correct one.

The point involved here may be put differently by saying that we must distinguish between two uses of 'define'. It can mean either 'provide a verbal equivalent for . . .' or 'give the ordinary use of . . .' To define in the first sense is to provide a word or a number of words which can be substituted for the word in question without affecting the truth or falsehood of any sentence in which that word occurs. It is frequently convenient because the substituted words may be more common or simpler than the original word. To define in the second sense is to give instances of sentences in which the relevant word is used and thereby clear up its logical function.

Thus it is correct to say 'He believes passionately that . . .' but not 'He knows passionately that . . .'. But to state this is not to contribute anything to the verbal definition of 'know' or 'believe'.

Now when we attend to 'defining' in this sense, we see that it is no matter for surprise that the uses, that is, the meanings of words change from time to time and that some words cease to be useful and are either discarded altogether or are given or acquire new and sometimes quite different uses; and it is important to notice some of the ways in which this can happen since failure to do so leads to much unnecessary mystification in political thinking.

Probably the best and the commonest reason we have for giving up words and for changing their use is that we make discoveries about the nature of the world, and a simple instance of this may be found in the history of some technical scientific words like 'phlogiston' and 'ether'. These were invented to help in the explanation of chemical and physical occurrences, and it was believed that things or substances existed of which they were the names. Great efforts were made to establish experimentally the existence of such substances but none were successful. Not only were phlogiston and ether themselves unobservable, but it gradually became clear that no observable phenomena could be indicated whose occurrence could be explained only by postulating the existence of phlogiston or ether, since other and more acceptable hypotheses would provide the explanations required. Hence it was eventually admitted that these were useless words and they were generally dropped as worthless linguistic lumber. They still have meanings in the sense that they have verbal definitions. They can be looked up in the *Oxford English Dictionary*. But they have no meaning in the sense that they have no use. They are dead.

Such words are simple to dispose of because they are technical words. They were deliberately made up to do a special job, and as soon as it became clear either that there was no job for them to do or that they were badly qualified to do it, they could disappear without trace since they served no useful purpose. Words in common use are less easy to dispose of. Their looser texture gives them a better chance to survive and to acquire new uses.

Consider for instance the words 'ghost' and 'devil'. These resemble 'phlogiston' and 'ether' in that some of their uses have now disappeared. We no longer employ them as our ancestors did because we have discovered other and more satisfactory methods of explaining the occurrence of diseases, floods, neurotic affections, and hallucinations. But they are not dead in the sense in which 'phlogiston' and 'ether' are dead, since some people still claim to have a use for them. It is therefore important to notice what can profitably be asked about them, and this is not 'Do ghosts or devils exist?' but 'What are, or are alleged to be, the phenomena which we need "ghost" and "devil" to describe or explain, and which we cannot satisfactorily describe or explain without them or their synonyms?'

The point I wish to make here is well illustrated by the history of words like 'purpose' and 'free-will' during the past three and a half centuries. Descartes and his successors were moved by a very praiseworthy ambition to discard moribund and useless words. They saw clearly that 'occult essences' and 'substantial forms' were phrases which performed no useful work. You give me no explanation of anything when you tell me that opium sends me to sleep because it possesses a '*vis dormitiva*' or 'soporific potency'. The Cartesians therefore concentrated entirely on mechanical causes and had no use (except for purposes of theological appeasement) for 'purpose' and 'free-will' at all. This austerity was satisfactory enough as long as physics was the only science to be seriously and successfully pursued. We do not need 'purpose' or 'choice' to describe or explain the behaviour of the things with which physics has to deal. With the development of other sciences, however, it became an embarrassment. It is not convenient or even practicable to describe clearly the phenomena with which biology, psychology, and sociology are concerned if we restrict ourselves to the language which is suitable for describing machines. Hence 'choice', 'purpose' and other words of the same family were gradually and somewhat apologetically reintroduced, though many of their earlier implications were dropped. In the meantime, however, much time and energy had been devoted to such questions as 'What is the essence of free-will, life, and purpose?', 'Does free-will exist?', and so on, when what should have been asked was 'What observable human and animal behaviour do we need "free-will" to describe or explain?' In politics 'natural rights' is a phrase which has developed in much the same way as 'free-will', while instances of discarded or moribund words and phrases are readily available in 'divine right', 'royal authority', and others, which purport to designate the essential character of kings or rulers, that is, their magical or supernatural status.

There is another way in which the use of words tends to be altered. The facts themselves may change and verbaᵢ usage has to be accommodated to them. This is particularly important in politics since the character of human associations tends to change fairly rapidly. A good instance here is provided by the use of 'own'. In ordinary language there is nothing obscure or complicated about 'John owns that watch' or 'That watch belongs to John'. We understand by them that John can use the watch, give it away, break it, and generally do what he likes with it provided he does not use it as a missile against other people. The police will do nothing to stop him and will do something to stop anyone who interferes with him. In fact everything is perfectly simple as long as most of the things in which people are interested belong to somebody in this straightforward way. But soon the situation becomes more complex. We have joint ownership to deal with, and then limited liability companies, nationalization, and so on. And at this point we are liable to get puzzled and to suppose that questions like 'Who now owns Oxford Railway Station?' present a philosophical difficulty. We feel that there ought to be someone who is related to Oxford Railway Station in the same way as that in which John is related to his watch, for 'X owns Oxford Railway Station' is the form of a correct English sentence. Yet if we complete it and say 'The State owns Oxford Railway Station' something seems to have gone wrong and we are tempted to ask 'And who is the person called "the State"?', 'Does such a person really exist?', 'Is he very rich?', and so on. But this worry has no substance. The correct answer is that in the sense in which John owns his watch nobody owns Oxford Railway Station. The factual situation is perfectly clear. It is that in fairly advanced political and economic associations it is found more convenient to have some goods and services controlled by persons appointed by the central government than to leave the disposal of them in the hands of private individuals.

It is primarily the job of lawyers to decide what is the most convenient linguistic device for dealing with this situation. It can be dealt with either by inventing a new technical word or by stretching the use of a word already familiar. Usually the second method is preferred, partly because it avoids more confusion than it creates, indeed it seldom confuses anybody but political philosophers, and partly because the extended use has often come to be adopted uncritically in the natural course of events. There is therefore nothing wrong with 'The State owns Oxford Railway Station', provided this is recognized as describing in an abbreviated way a rather complicated fact about British economic and political organization. It does not imply that the Monarch or the Prime Minister or anybody else can blow Oxford Railway Station up or give it away if they choose to do so, and it is purely a matter of convenience whether we choose to use 'own' like this as well as in the simpler sense (but without some of the implications of the simpler sense), or whether we coin a new word to do the job. All that matters is that there is not a person meant by 'The State' about whom we have to prosecute enquiries.

So much trouble has been caused by questions like 'Who owns Oxford Railway Station?' that it is worth studying another of them in order to get the situation quite clear. 'To whom do you owe your Income Tax?' is quite a good specimen. Here again ordinary usage is not obscure. 'Owe' is the sort of word which occurs in statements such as 'A owes B ten pounds'. We need the names of two people and of a thing or sum of money to fit it into a grammatical sentence, and usually we also want to add 'for something', e.g. for a pair of shoes. But to whom does Mr Jones owe his Income Tax and what does he owe it for? The short and correct answer is that he owes it to the State for social, defence, and other services of various kinds. But it has still to be remembered that 'The State' is not the name of a person and the social services are not things or actions which can be precisely specified as a pair of shoes or the services of a caddy for a round of golf can be. There is nothing contradictory in saying that your insurance company has done nothing for you in a year in which you make no claims and also that it has done something in that it has insured you, and you owe it money for doing so. Again we have the situation in which the use of an existing word has been stretched to meet a new factual development. We get into trouble only if we suppose that this verbal usage has brought into existence new and peculiar people and things, the ghosts of those which the old usage required. Linguistic conveniences do not beget metaphysical entities, though it is fatally easy to suppose that they do, especially if we accept the doctrine that words have meanings in the classical sense.

The upshot of this is that the search for the true or correct meaning or use of words and sentences is a wild goose chase. There are no such uses except in the trivial sense in which a foreigner or a child may be ignorant of the correct use of English expressions. This, however, does not commit us to the position of Humpty Dumpty. There are indeed no fixed immutable or essential meanings or concepts, but for all that verbal usage at any given time and for any given society is fairly stable and is not subject to the arbitrary whims of individuals. This is not surprising and no cosmological or theological explanation of it is called for. Verbal usage is stable because the objects and situations with which people are confronted and which they need to describe, discuss, and alter, are also fairly stable. They resemble one another in many ways and tend to resemble themselves at different times. There is, however, very seldom any single element in such resemblances which is identical as between different individuals or in the same individual at different times. Hence there is no single test which will decide whether a word like 'State' is being correctly used, and the same is true of 'justice', 'temperance', and the rest. The position is rather that at any given time there is a number of tests, and it is not necessary that all of them should be passed. What we have to deal with is a matter of more or less and not, as classical theory would have it, a straightforward 'either . . . or' disjunction.

Thus a particular piece of legislation may be correctly described as 'just' in that it places financial burdens on those who are now best able to carry them, but unjust in that it penalizes those who have in the past been provident and thrifty as compared with those who have been careless and extravagant. There are many other factors which may also be taken into account, and a great deal of one of them may counterbalance a little each of a lot of others. A little unfairness may be accepted if a great deal of good is brought about. Thus the reason why Socrates nearly always failed and admitted that he had failed in his search for the true meaning of political words was that there was no such meaning to be discovered, in spite of the fact that the people to whom he talked used these words in an intelligent way and understood one another without difficulty. The uses were not precise like those of some technical words, but they were, and are, of the proper level of precision for purposes of communication in the world in which we happen to live. A different kind of world would require a different kind of linguistic equipment. But when Plato in the *Republic* claimed to have discovered the essence of justice, what he did was to concentrate exclusively on one usage, that of sticking to your own job and not interfering

with other people in the performance of theirs, and this proceeding, because it was not in accordance with normal
usage, inevitably led him into paradoxical statements. The
precise and the normal imprecise usages were incompatible
with one another.

§3. *The illusion of absolute standards*

The suggestion that the traditional questions 'What is the
State?', 'What is justice?', and so on, are unprofitable is
not readily acceptable to many who rightly respect the contribution made by Plato to the development of Western
philosophy. Even if it is agreed that the criticism of the
Platonic theory of meaning put forward in the preceding
section is largely justified, there is a further argument, also
Platonic in origin, which requires consideration before the
well-entrenched belief that political philosophy is directed
to the investigation of the ideas of the State, Justice, and
Liberty can be confidently abandoned.

The argument in question runs as follows. It is clearly
significant to say that A is taller or stronger or a better
carpenter than B, yet it would make no sense to compare in
this way unless we had some norm or standard by which to
judge. Furthermore, such a standard must be absolute. It
cannot itself be subject to measurement or we should have
an indefinite regress, since it would again be possible to ask
'By what standard of measurement are we judging?', and
so on indefinitely. Applying this argument to politics, we
find that one type of political institution cannot significantly be called superior to another type unless both can be
compared with some ideal, unchallengeable standard; it is
only by discovering that one of our specimens approxi-
mates more closely to this standard than the other does that
we can adjudicate between them.

It is a sign of the relative backwardness of the social
sciences as compared with physics, chemistry, and biology,
that this argument is still often taken seriously in the former

though it has long been abandoned in practice, and more recently in principle, by the latter. In practice it was discarded by the inventors of modern scientific methods of investigation. Galileo, for instance, in his early experiments made use of his pulse beats for measuring small intervals of time. One day an earth tremor shook the church in which he happened to be and caused the lamps to swing. Checking his observations against his pulse beats he found that the swings took equal times, and this suggested to him that a pendulum would be a more convenient and more reliable measure of time than his pulse beats were; and the development of this idea led to the production of the pendulum clock.

Since then other and more precise methods have been devised in order to make more accurate observations possible, and it is perhaps tempting to argue that Galileo and his successors must surely have been in possession of the Idea of an Absolute Standard of time-measurement or they could not have noted either that existing standards were imperfect or that one of them was superior to the others. Yet it is difficult to see that such seemingly profound pronouncements tell us anything at all, for we may well ask what it is like to possess or to contemplate an absolute standard of measurement for time or indeed for anything whatever. How should we know that such a standard could never be improved upon? Certainly neither Galileo nor any of his successors in designing chronometers have ever suggested that they had such a standard, much less that they had to have it in order to regulate their watches. It is not sensible to say that nobody but a master in any subject is competent to give instruction in the elements of it.

What happens in practice is quite easy to state and to understand. It involves no reference to ideal or absolute standards, and nothing but the hypnotism of words leads to the supposition that it does. We make improvements piecemeal in accordance with our needs of the moment. We try new gadgets to see whether they will help us, and if they do, we adopt them and try some more. Sometimes we attempt to look further ahead than the immediate future, but not often and not very far; and this is partly because we cannot see very far and partly because we should gain little or nothing if we could see better. The experiments with which Galileo and Newton were concerned did not need complicated chronometers to make them possible. A quartz clock, even if scientists could conceivably have thought of it, would have been of no use in such experiments since it was the movements of relatively large and slow-moving objects like the planets which required to be measured and for these a very simple technique was perfectly adequate.

It is true that many physicists continued to pay attention to the idea of absolute standards and other metaphysical ideas in theory while ignoring them in their experimental practice. They had no need to worry themselves about what metaphysicians asserted to be the foundations or presuppositions of their science, but they often did so, and were puzzled by paradoxes arising from accepted definitions of 'space', 'time', 'absolute motion', and so on. But these were not, and are not, difficulties within physics. They neither helped nor hindered discoveries about electricity, magnetism, or the kinetic theory of gases.

In comparatively recent times a further step has been taken. Since Einstein's general theory of relativity has been universally accepted it has also been clear that the ideas of absolute space and time and therefore that of absolute measurement are strictly meaningless, that is, they contribute nothing to the description or explanation of any physical phenomena; and these ideas have accordingly been abandoned without embarrassment.

Up to a point the notion of absolute standards in politics has had a similar history. Plato, Rousseau, and many others have claimed to give us or make explicit to us ideal standards of political institutions with which existing systems could be compared, but what they have in fact done is almost exactly what Galileo did. They have considered the actual institutions available to them for study and have suggested some more or less radical alterations in them. Plato seems to have held that the constitution of Sparta was on the whole satisfactory, though it would be better if some, but not all, of the culture of Athens could be grafted on to it; Rousseau with some important qualifications was happy enough with the constitution of Geneva. What else indeed should they or could they have done? Yet in political philosophy the belief that they did, or might have done more, still lingers on. It is not so powerful as it once was but it is kept alive partly by tradition and partly by the acceptance of another mistaken doctrine which has now to be considered.

§4. *The illusion of geometrical method*

The argument which has to be met here may be stated in the following way. The triangles we draw on pieces of paper are never quite right. Their sides are never quite straight, their angles are never strictly angles, and the sum of them is never precisely equal to 180°. Nevertheless, the reasonings of Euclid are cogent. Therefore it cannot be about triangles on pieces of paper that he is reasoning, though he is certainly telling us truths about triangles. Hence it seems fair to suppose that he is talking about real or ideal triangles of which those drawn on paper are inferior copies. It must therefore, the argument runs, be admitted that in geometry we are concerned with ideals, and since geometrical truths are discovered by the study of ideals, it is reasonable to suppose that political truths may be discovered by the same method. The process of discovery here may indeed be more difficult both because the subject matter is more complicated and because we seldom if ever approach political questions with the dispassionate interest that we normally take in geometry; but these are not good reasons for doubting the efficacy of the method. That is approximately the classical argument. It is mistaken, but the mistake was almost un-avoidable at the time when it was first made. There is, however, no justification at all for adhering to it now.

The first approximation to a more correct statement of the situation is to say that Euclidean geometry is not about triangles at all. It is simply a postulational system in which some axioms and rules of inference are laid down and con-clusions are derived by means of them. It is equally possible to choose different axioms and get different conclusions. We can modify the axiom of parallels if we want to, and a geo-metry radically different from that of Euclid but equally consistent will be the result. In neither case do ideal figures come into the story, for the story is not about figures. It is simply the manipulation of symbols in accordance with recognized rules of transformation. It is, however, not at all obvious that this is the case, for the Euclidean manipulation certainly yields practical results. Surveyors and engineers actually get the right answers within the limits of accuracy with which they are concerned by making Euclidean calcu-lations, and it is therefore natural to maintain that Euclid-ean geometry is in some important sense right and that alternative systems giving different results would be wrong. So it looks as if Euclid's axioms were after all statements of essential truths about matter of fact and not just con-venient assumptions, and then it is natural to argue that since we have such *a priori* or intuitive insight into the frame-work of the physical universe we may reasonably claim to have it also about human institutions like the State.

But this is still a mistaken doctrine. Of course axioms are not just selected at random. They are adopted because they are expected to work, that is, it is discovered by experience that calculations made from them will give results which are true about matter of fact. What is at first sight odd about the Euclidean axioms is simply that they are so easy to formulate, that they work for so many purposes, and that they can be pressed as hard as they can be without breaking down. Even this is not really very surprising. They are the axioms which creatures with our kind of perceptual apparatus might be expected to invent, and our perceptual apparatus has been evolved because it has survival value for creatures of that kind of shape and size living in this sort of world.

But we should not be deceived by this into supposing that these axioms state necessary or universal truths about matter of fact. No postulational system can do that. Even if we had not yet discovered experimentally the point at which calculations based on Euclidean axioms failed to give reliable predictions, we should be justified in expecting that such a point would be reached sooner or later. In fact it has now been reached. Deductions from Euclidean axioms do not give reliable predictions for particles travelling at approximately the speed of light. To describe these a different geometry is required.

What all this comes to is that there is really a double error in the view that political philosophy is the same sort of enquiry as geometry. In the first place the nature of geometry is misconceived. It is not an *a priori* study of the structure of the real world but a postulational system whose applicability to matter of fact is extensive but limited. Nobody could say in advance where the limit would be, and it was therefore mistaken but not reprehensible to suppose that there was no limit. We now know where the limit comes, and also what to do when we reach it. In fact, geometry is either *a priori*, in which case it is not about matter of fact at all, or it is about matter of fact, and then it is just a set of ordinary empirical hypotheses which can be tested and disproved.

In the second place the analogy between geometry and politics is a very weak one even when the nature of geometry is properly stated. It is true but not helpful to say that dictatorship is the natural form of government for creatures which take a long time to reach maturity and which need quick but intelligent decisions if they are to escape destruction by faster and better armed opponents. This is possibly good enough to account for the behaviour of savages, but no reliable calculations can be drawn from it about civilized society. It is at best a feasible hypothesis but a very unfruitful one. The same is true of the comparison of human associations with organic bodies. There are some points of resemblance, but as compared with the axioms of Euclid this and other axioms concerning politics are pitifully useless.

§5. *What classical political philosophy is about*

This general discussion of the beliefs which governed Greek political thought is necessary because these beliefs have been and still are the basis of nearly all the enquiries which are generally called 'political philosophy'. Unless they are shown to be mistaken, as I have tried to show them to be, those enquiries still have a claim to be taken seriously and to be prosecuted further in the hope that they will eventually lead to the discovery of truth. For Plato had clearly some justification for maintaining that if there is a world of Ideas which is in some way the foundation of the world which we commonly call real then we ought to endeavour to investigate it.

The view I want to put, however, is that there is strictly no sense in this Platonic doctrine. There is nothing behind or beyond actual political institutions which those institutions express, copy, or realize. The supposition that there is derives largely from the assumptions I have already criticized, but it is reinforced by a series of confusions between historical, scientific, and linguistic propositions which I shall now consider.

Let us begin by taking some of the best known pronouncements of classical political philosophers and some of the questions which occur most frequently in examination papers on political philosophy.

'Justice is the interest of the stronger' *Thrasymachus.*
'The State is by nature prior to the individual' *Aristotle.*
'Covenants without the Sword are but words' *Hobbes.*
'We hold it as self-evident that all men are created free and

equal and are endowed by their Creator with certain inalienable rights among which are life, liberty, and the pursuit of happiness' *Declaration of Independence*.

'The State is a committee for managing the affairs of the bourgeois class as a whole' *Communist Manifesto*.

'Will, not force, is the basis of the State' *T. H. Green*.

The following are fair samples of questions:

Are there any natural rights?
Whence is the authority of the State derived?
Is there a social contract?
Is liberty promoted or restricted by the rule of law?

We are so accustomed to this sort of pronouncement and this type of question that we seldom enquire further into their *bona fides*. Yet if we do look more closely at them they present some very puzzling features.

The main point is this. There are many fields of enquiry in which the Greeks and the investigators of the seventeenth and eighteenth centuries were unable to reach any satisfactory conclusions but which are now no longer unexplored. The size and distance away from us of the stars, electricity, the constitution of matter, and the generation of living organisms are all in this class. How is it then that no progress whatever has been made in answering the questions which Plato and Aristotle formulated about States, justice, and liberty? Possibly they are extremely difficult, like a gigantic crossword or jig-saw puzzle, but even so one would expect that the efforts of a great many intelligent men over two and a half thousand years would have produced some definite and accepted results. At least a few of the bits ought to have been fitted together so that there is no room for further argument about them. Yet this is not the case. It is possible to say that the questions of political philosophy unlike those of science are eternal questions which every generation of men must propound and answer anew. But this though it is solemn is not illuminating. It admits failure without giving any reason for it.

For the trouble about the traditional questions in

political philosophy is that we do not know how to set about looking for answers to them, and the real trouble about the pronouncements is that we do not know what kind of evidence we should need to demonstrate that they are either true or false. In fact, we do not know what kind of investigation it is that political philosophers have pursued, and therefore we find it impossible to decide whether they have pursued it skilfully or clumsily. We do not know whether they have ignored relevant evidence because we do not know what sort of evidence was relevant to the purpose they had in view.

It seems clear that we are not concerned here with a historical investigation. 'The State is by nature prior to the individual' is not at all like 'George IV was prior to William IV'. We do not look for documentary or archaeological evidence to establish or refute it. 'Is there a social contract?' is a different sort of question from 'Did Caesar leave his property to the citizens of Rome?' We may not know the answer to the second of these, but we know the kind of evidence we should want to satisfy us about it, and we also know that this kind of evidence would not be relevant to answering the first question even though some philosophers have half suggested that it would be. Hobbes at any rate knew better than that.

But scientific enquiry does not seem to be involved either. 'All men are born free' is not like 'All men are born white'. We could refute the latter by pointing to a black baby. But babies are not born with labels on them saying 'Slave' or 'Free', or even 'Prince' or 'Commoner'. Aristotle almost regretted that they were not, but had to admit that parentage was not a reliable guide to status in the special sense in which he was interested in it. Equally we should not refute 'Covenants without the sword are but words' by showing that Smith paid his tailor's bill without being threatened by the police, and we should not conduct a series of controlled experiments to prove that will and not force is the basis of the State.

The Logic of the Classical Theories

But if neither historical nor scientific enquiry is involved, is the whole business simply a discussion about linguistic usage? Have we just to compare a number of deductive systems none of which has anything to do with matter of fact except by accident and from which no factual conclusions can be reached? If this is the case it is not surprising that no answers to the questions of politics have been discovered, for in the nature of the case no answers can be discovered. To ask whether Hobbes or Hegel or Marx was right would be as pointless as to ask whether the axioms of Euclid or those of Riemann or Lobachevsky are right, and we have already seen that this sort of question is devoid of sense. Unquestionably a lot of discussion which is called political philosophy is on just this level. It has no factual content and is simply argument about verbal definitions. This does not mean that it has no practical importance, but it does mean that there is no method of proving one view to be correct and the other false; and this is not because the proof is very difficult to discover and formulate like the geometrical proof of the volume of a sphere, but that it makes no sense to talk about proof in this connexion. You cannot disprove the rules of whist by citing those of bridge, for rules are not the kind of things which can be proved or disproved any more than they can be eaten or worn.

This conclusion is important, but it needs further elucidation, since it is easy to make too little and too much of it when estimating the significance of classical political philosophers. Hobbes and Locke provide between them a notably clear and straightforward instance of what is involved. Both of them were concerned to recommend the adoption of new definitions of political terms. Hobbes believed in absolutism and strong government. Hence he wanted to make it a contradiction to talk about limited or constitutional monarchy. His entire system is dependent on the axiom that the monarch has no responsibility for his acts except in the very vague sense that he is ultimately bound to answer to God for what he does. It is true that the absolute character of monarchy is not explicitly stated as an axiom, but the contractual story on which it is based is too obviously fictitious to be taken seriously. At best it represents a sweeping psychological hypothesis about human beings, and at worst it is just a fraud. In fact, the ruler is defined as a dictator and the consequences of this definition are expounded. Locke, on the other hand, writes deliberately to support the Glorious Revolution of 1688. Hence his definition of 'ruler' is quite different. Only a constitutional monarch is genuine. He has definite obligations to his subjects and if he ignores these he is rightly expelled.

Stated in this way the contribution of Hobbes and Locke may sound rather trivial. It seems as if verbal recommendations of this kind do not matter much. But they do. Any alteration in the rules of a game is a redefinition. It is not a fact of nature but the consequence of a piece of arbitrary definition that you cannot be out to a no-ball or score a try off a forward pass. Yet some redefinitions seriously affect the chances of one side against another. For suppose that you are especially strong in left-handed players and that you have developed a special technique for training and using them. It is evident that your chances of winning matches would be seriously affected by a rule prohibiting their participation in the game, yet logically this would merely be a redefinition of 'batsman', 'bowler', and 'fieldsman'. Similarly it seems a trivial matter whether a tree is defined as a growth more than six feet high and a shrub as anything shorter than that. But it may make a great deal of difference to the owners if a rule is made to the effect that all trees in a particular area are to be felled and all shrubs left standing. In exactly the same way it is from one point of view a trivial matter whether we choose to define 'monarch' as 'absolute ruler' or as 'ruler in accordance with the constitution', but it makes a great deal of difference when 'monarch' is already embodied in constitutional law or when it is proposed to make new laws in accordance with the revised definition.

All this is correct as far as it goes and it is a fatal mistake to ignore it. The greater part of classical political philosophy really is concerned with recommending and providing worthless logical grounds for the adoption or perpetuation of axioms and definitions involving political words like 'State', 'law', and 'rights'. And the practical results of adopting the recommended redefinitions are often important, though the redefinitions themselves are no more puzzling than are alterations in the rules of bridge or football.

But this is not the whole truth. Radical positivists tend to make the same sort of mistake here as they have sometimes made about the sciences. As we have seen, an important element in Einstein's general theory of relativity was that it dispensed with the notion of absolute space, time, matter, and motion in physics. The questions 'What *is* space?' and so on were therefore recognized as meaningless. Instead of talking about space we talk about spatial co-ordinates, and these are purely conventional. We can have as many as we find it convenient to have in order to describe adequately what happens, for co-ordinates do not exist in the sense in which trees and tables exist. It is natural but mistaken to extend this very important piece of doctrine and to say that all science is purely conventional and that it is concerned solely with discovering convenient linguistic tricks. To talk in such a way, however, is extremely misleading since the position is really more like this. A great many things happen in the world such as eclipses, railway accidents, economic depressions, and wars. It is important to us to understand what is happening, to explain what has happened, and to predict what is going to happen. Ordinary languages and calculi like formal logic, geometry, and arithmetic are devices we have invented to facilitate such understanding, explanation, and prediction. It was formerly thought that they could perform their function only if they consisted of models or copies of reality, but this belief has been shown to be mistaken. Hence in one sense the decision as to what calculi and what syntax we shall adopt is wholly arbitrary. We may please ourselves about it. In another sense it is not so, since languages and calculi may be clumsily constructed or unwisely selected. They may encourage us to make false predictions or to act incompetently. In other words we may select any system of co-ordinates or equations which we find convenient for discussing or describing events in nature, but these systems are not truths about the world. The casualties in a railway accident are not increased or reduced by the language, whether technical or not, in which it is reported. There is no valid argument from truths about notation to truths about matter of fact.

The position in political philosophy is similar but a little more complicated. Here too it was correctly noted by the early positivists of the Vienna Circle in the 1920's that a great deal of argument which purported to be about matter of fact was in truth no more than wrangling about conventional definitions. As we have already noted, we need not deny that important practical results may flow from the adoption of one definition rather than another. For instance it may be agreed that all men have a natural right to life, liberty, and the pursuit of happiness, but 'man' may be so defined as to exclude Negroes. Abraham Lincoln and many others have observed this possibility. But no factual discovery is reported by this kind of exercise. Hence the temptation to say that the classical political philosophers were occupied with logic chopping, often with a view to underwriting more or less disreputable politics, *and with nothing else*. Yet this account, though it contains a lot of important truth, will not bear examination. For, if we say that political philosophy is concerned solely with linguistic usage, we can be convicted of talking nonsense by an argument like this.

Suppose that in Nazi Germany you had set out to discover the German equivalents of English words of appraisal, 'good', 'honest', 'praiseworthy', 'treacherous', and so on.

You would have learnt that the correct usage was '*schön*', '*ehrlich*', '*ehrenwert*', '*unehrlich*', and so on. Further you would have found that the German words had the same inference licenses attached to them as the English ones. If you were *ehrlich* you were likely to get a decoration, if you were *unehrlich* you were likely to go to a concentration camp. So far, so good. But then you might have seen a S.A. man (or a lot of them) beating up a Jew and you might have said '*Das ist verbrecherisch*'. Your teacher would have said '*Durchaus nicht verbrecherisch. Eine ehrenwerte Tat*'. And what could you say then? You might accept the correction in the same way as that in which in the United States you accept the correction 'We don't call them braces, we call them suspenders, and what you call suspenders, we call garters'. But if you did your friends would not have said 'You have learnt German very well'. They would have said 'You are a liar and a hypocrite. You know it is wicked to behave like that, yet you are saying that it is praiseworthy. You are pretending in order to avoid trouble'.

One way out of this embarrassment is to say that words of appraisal are not descriptive at all. They are just exclamations like 'Hurrah!' Another is to say that they are descriptive but describe not the factual situation but the psychological state of the speaker. For reasons which will appear later neither of these will do; indeed one may say at this stage that both are clearly false. When I say 'That is wicked' I am at least trying to make a reliable report about the world and not one about my own emotional condition.

But it will not do either to say that appraisal words have the same job to do as the symbols used by mathematicians and physicists. They have a fact-reporting function, though it is not what we usually take it to be. 'That is good' does not report the presence of a quality as 'That is white' does. I shall try to give a better analysis of it in Chapter V. For the moment I am concerned with what it was that classical political philosophers were trying to do, which is not notational disputation. All of them were trying to describe the political institutions which they considered praiseworthy, and they were perfectly right to do this, for political institutions are just as factual as railway accidents and some of them are in a perfectly intelligible sense praiseworthy. They also wanted to give reasons for preferring one set of institutions to another, and this was correct too, though it was not strictly a philosophical exercise. Where they went wrong was in looking for the wrong kind of reasons; more accurately they aimed at getting not reasons but proofs. They asked wrong and even senseless questions because, on the assumption they accepted, those questions looked sensible, and in the background there was always the alarming but unjustified suspicion that if those questions were really not sensible it would follow that all political and all moral appraisals were purely conventional, so that in the end we should have to say 'The Russians or the Germans call this "good" but we don't, and that is all there is to be said about it'. Yet we know perfectly well that the trouble at the moment between the U.S.S.R. and the United States is not that there is a shortage of competent interpreters. It is true that if I say 'Look, there is a man' and you reply 'No, it's a scarecrow' you may be correcting my English; but it is much more probable that you are challenging my discernment.

So far I have dealt in generalities, which are never convincing. I shall now proceed to consider in detail the actual use of political words. This will I hope show more clearly both what I think is wrong with the traditional approach to them and what questions can profitably be asked by philosophers about political institutions and organization. I shall then criticize what I consider to be the myths of totalitarianism, democracy, and communism to which the classical method of reasoning has given rise and shall finally show that these criticisms do not lead to any perilous scepticism or subjectivism about the political institutions of Britain or the United States.

CHAPTER 3

The Uses of Political Words

§1. *Introduction*

THE words whose uses I shall discuss and try to elucidate in this chapter are 'State', 'authority', 'rights', 'law', and 'liberty'. Before I examine them individually, there are some comments which apply to all of them. I have already given reasons for maintaining that questions of the form 'What is the State?' and 'Do rights exist?' are unprofitable. They look like 'What is the Albert Memorial?' and 'Do dodos exist?' yet it is clear that the resemblance is only superficial. We settle the latter by looking them up in an encyclopedia. If further evidence is required we undertake journeys of exploration to Kensington or Mauritius. But this will not do for States and rights, for these political words are not the names of persons or things at all. They describe an aspect of human behaviour, the way in which human beings get themselves organized for some particular purpose.

Furthermore these and other words of the same family are dependent on one another. From 'X is a member of a State' it is legitimate to infer that he has some rights, is subject to some laws, is amenable to some authority and enjoys some liberty. We should certainly withdraw 'He is a member of a State' if all these conclusions were shown to be false. Whether all of them imply one another or not is less clear. What is apparent and important however is that 'He has rights' etc. do not imply 'He is a member of a State', but only 'He is a member of some association or other'. Hence it would perhaps be technically better to drop 'State' and substitute 'association'. I shall have more to say on this point shortly. For the moment it is sufficient to remark that the predominant concern of classical philosophy with the words I have selected is a sufficient reason

45

for choosing them even though there are objections to them, and it must be remembered throughout that their uses overlap so that they cannot be analysed without reference to one another except by a rather rough but convenient process of abstraction.

§2. '*The State*'

The confident and uncritical way in which 'the State' is used by many modern writers suggests that 'State' is the same sort of word as 'water', 'mountain', or 'sun'. It is easy to see that this is a mistake. There is no reason to doubt that when Cicero wrote '*aqua*', '*mons*', or '*sol*', he was referring to things indistinguishable for practical purposes from those to which we refer by 'water', 'mountain', and 'sun'. But 'State' is not in the same way equivalent to '*respublica*' or '*civitas*'. Human institutions, as we have noted in considering 'own' and 'owe', change more rapidly and radically than physical objects.

'State' as might be expected on historical grounds is not even a very old word in English. It dates, as far as the usage in which we are interested is concerned, only from the middle of the sixteenth century. It then sometimes stands for what we now call 'the Government' or 'the rulers', the modern Marxist use as will appear later, and sometimes, less precisely, it is roughly equivalent to 'commonwealth' or 'polity'. In the second of these uses it inherits a good many associations, some of them mystical or supernatural from the Greek '*Polis*' and '*Politeia*' as well as from the Roman '*Respublica*' and the medieval 'Empire' and 'Monarchy'. It is only in the seventeenth and eighteenth centuries that it acquires technical or semi-technical status as a legal and political term.

These are elementary points, but it is wise to bear them in mind since much of the apparent obscurity and real confusion involved in questions about the State occur only because they are neglected in the search for real meanings.

To-day, however, we all know how to use 'the State' in ordinary speech. The U.S.S.R. is certainly a State. So is Switzerland. Surrey is certainly not a State. Nor is U.N.O. But there are cases in which we are liable to become uncertain. Is Liechtenstein a State? or New York? There is nothing mystifying about this uncertainty, and we know how to remove it. International lawyers have created a technical usage for 'State' and have elaborated tests for deciding whether a particular association belongs to this class. 'Is Liechtenstein a State?' is just like 'Is the whale a fish?' The correct answer in both cases is to be found in books of reference. What then does it mean to say 'I don't think Leichtenstein is really a State' or 'I don't think the whale is really a fish'? I may mean either of two things. (1) That it does not satisfy the tests. The definition says that the term 'State' or 'fish' should be used if and only if certain tests are passed. In the case of 'State' the lawyers say these are independence, geographical definition, some standards of organization and so on, and it may be that Liechtenstein fails to pass some of them. In the case of 'fish' the biologists say they are coldness of blood and so on, and the whale does fail to pass some of these. Provided the technical terms are devised with reasonable skill and care, there is no difficulty in this sort of case. If they are not, what is needed is a conference of experts or a recognized court of some kind to settle the matter. (2) Verbal usage may not be in dispute, but I may be suggesting that it is inconvenient or misleading. I may agree that Liechtenstein passes the test but consider that it differs from the U.S.S.R. in such important ways that it is confusing to locate both of them in the same class. This is the same sort of thing as to say 'A tortoise isn't really an insect, even though it may be classified in that way by the Railway Company'. 'State' then has a vague but convenient ordinary use and a precise, technical, legal use. Has it any other use which can be called philosophical? I do not think it has. With some reservation which will appear when the idealist theory of the State is under discussion it seems to me that all the relevant phenomena can be fully described without further complication.

There are, however, two points which need to be cleared up if this account is to be acceptable. First there are what I have called the mystical overtones. It is undeniable that from the days of Greece onwards States have tended to be personified. Their names have often been linked with those of deities and their rulers have been credited with divine or semi-divine sanctity and power. It remained for some writers in the nineteenth and twentieth centuries to deify the State itself, that is to pretend that 'Britain' or 'Gross-Deutschland' is the name of a kind of supernatural person with superhuman attributes. This pretence was dangerously misleading and in so far as it is still an ingredient in the popular use of 'the State' it should be abandoned in the same way that the magical ingredients in 'life', 'force', and 'matter' have now been abandoned. Even as metaphors they are unsafe and we are much better off without them.

The second point is more important. It is often argued that 'State' is not merely a term standing for one type of association but also that this one type of association is unique and not at all like cricket clubs, trade unions, or even Churches. Many reasons have been advanced for maintaining this, but only three of them have sufficient plausibility to deserve attention. The first is that of involuntary membership. It is argued that if I do not like my cricket club or my trade union or even my Church, I can resign from it and join a different one. But I cannot escape from my State in this way. There seems to me to be very little in this. At most there is a difference of degree, and even this is difficult to establish at all firmly. Resigning from any institution involves some inconvenience. This is usually minimal in cricket clubs and very considerable in trade unions. In the case of Churches it has sometimes been lethal. But to say that one cannot escape from one's State is simply untrue. Normally emigration is possible, though it is sometimes so difficult as to be practically out of the question. But there is always suicide, and it is not in these days so very un-common.

The second argument which is also unconvincing is that the State is concerned with the whole of our lives whereas other associations concern only part of them. But even if this is true, does it matter? It is not true except in a rather trivial sense. In modern times we tend to be bothered a good deal by State regulations. People do sometimes shoot themselves to avoid filling in any more forms for the Ministry of Agriculture. They are not, however, a very sub-stantial minority and most of us are little worried by the omnipresence of the State. It is equally trivial to say that the State makes culture or 'the good life' possible. Perhaps it is more important in this respect than other types of association, but this is highly dubitable. It looks plausible only if 'State' is defined so widely as to embrace all types of association. Finally it may be maintained that the State is qualitatively different or of a different order from other types of association since it determines their legality and therefore makes it possible for them to exist at all. This has force only if we fail to distinguish between legal and factual existence. There is a sense in which the Roman Catholic Church or the Communist Party could be abolished in this country by legislation, but there is another and much more important one in which they could not. The legal non-existence of the Communist Party in Tsarist Russia did not prevent the Bolshevist Revolution of 1917.

In fact I think these poor reasons are adduced because of an unconscious addiction to the mystical residue. It is felt that 'State' ought to designate something different in kind from cricket clubs and trade unions. Hence an effort is made to show that Britain and the rest really do have some-thing which other types of association do not have. The attempt seems to me to be unnecessary and unsuccessful.

It is sometimes suggested however that while 'State' is the word for one association among others, 'Society' or 'the Community' stand for something different. It is in this something that we find wholes which are more than the sums of their parts (whatever that is supposed to mean) super-persons, transcendent unities, and so on. There really is a difference between 'State' and 'Society', but it is not philosophically important and not at all what the exponents of Social Solidarity would like it to be. 'Society' is used to stand for something less organized than an association. We talk more here of customs, habits, and traditions and less of rights, laws, and obligations. The position is not yet formalized and the relations between individuals are not clearly defined. But there is no hard and fast line to be drawn, as is indicated by the fact that in ordinary speech 'association' and 'society' are interchangeable words. It is perhaps convenient to make a technical distinction of this kind between less and more highly organized groups of people, but there seems to be nothing more to it than that. We do not need the fiction of a social contract to explain the transition from society to State.

The only other points of interest about 'State' are concerned with its connexion with the other political words and will arise as these are discussed.

§3. *'Authority'*

'Power' and 'Authority' are clearly connected with one another closely. Much unnecessary difficulty has arisen because their logical grammar has been commonly misconstrued. We use them correctly only when we recognize that they are not the names of two different but related entities of which one somehow depends on the other. It is misleading to say of anyone that his use of power depends on or is derived from his authority. What 'Jones is an authority on postage stamps' or 'drains' tells us is that on these matters people tend to accept what he says as true without pressing him for reasons. They do this because they have grounds for supposing that he could produce reasons if challenged. This usage resembles closely the ordinary use of 'authority' as a political word. Here too 'He has authority' has as an important ingredient 'People do what he tells them to do without asking questions.' Where this is truly asserted, it follows that he also has power. The Pope cannot put a lot of Divisions into the field, but the support of the Vatican is worth a lot of Divisions. Thus very roughly it may be said that to be in a position to exercise power or to use force in a certain way is to have authority. There are however many possibilities of confusion here and I shall try to elucidate some of them.

Until modern times the distinction between power and authority has not been at all clearly drawn and there is a strong magical element in both of them. Both power and authority have been thought of as conferred by the possession of a physical token or emblem of some sort. This both compels obedience and compels it rightly. If you are the Lord of the Ring, the Nibelungs have to dig gold for you. If you have the right talisman, the devils have to do as you tell them. But the ideas of bare force, force derived from a charm, and force rightly or justly applied, tend to overlap considerably. It is unnecessary to go into this idea here. It is linked with the general doctrine that rights depend on status and that status is something which can be acquired, inherited, or conferred.

The relevant fact is that from this point of view the question 'Whence is the authority of so and so derived?' is always a sensible and proper question. You can answer it by saying that it was conferred on him by some physical act like consecration or by the transfer of a sacred emblem or by the imparting of some closely guarded secret. As far as monarchs are concerned the intimate connexion between priests and kings made it very easy to maintain that the monarch's authority was derived from God and conferred on him by the priest with appropriate ritual. Again the details and controversies do not matter to us here; they are the concern of historians and anthropologists. The unquestioned assumption was and in political philosophy it often still is that 'Whence does the State derive its authority?' is a proper question. Broadly speaking two kinds of answer are propounded. The first is to accept the assumption in principle but to find a substitute for God and his priests as the conferring agency. Hence we get vague statements to the effect that the monarch (or the government) derives authority from the will of the people or the consent of the governed. 'Authority' changes its use in the standard way. It loses some mystical overtones and is used to designate something mundane and observable like elections, referenda, and majority decisions. But there still seem to be questions about the origins of authority to be considered. We want to know just what it is that is conferred on a person or Chamber by these devices. What does it mean to say that someone has exceeded his authority or lost it? How do we know that he possesses it?

This sort of question now seems odd and unanswerable. We can no longer produce the talisman or appeal to the coronation ritual. Hence there is always a temptation to simplify by dropping 'authority' altogether and maintaining that the only useful word in this sort of context is 'power'. Thrasymachus wanted to do this in Athens, and later on Machiavelli, Hobbes, Marx, and Austin have all been much influenced by the same notion. Yet it is not at all satisfactory. There are some acts which we wish to describe and for which 'authority' as distinct from 'power' is needed. We want to distinguish between the rightful and the wrongful employment of force. Hence 'authority' or a synonym always tends to creep back into use. Hobbes talks about the Law of Nature which is the Law of God though he cannot fit it into the set of ideas he wants to use, and Marx employs question-begging words like 'exploitation' which have no place in the kind of positivist account of political phenomena which he professes to offer us.

In fact, as I said at the start, the difficulty about 'authority' arises entirely because its logical grammar is not clearly understood. It is easy to see that this is the case if we stop for the moment talking about monarchs and States and attend to less solemn and more common uses of the word.

All sorts of people are commonly said to have authority. Referees, schoolmasters, N.C.O.s, and policemen are authorities. Yet we seldom or never ask where they get their authority from. It sounds a pointless question. We could say where they get their whistles, blackboards, and uniforms from. But clearly their authority is not like that. What then does it mean to say of some person or body that they have authority?

At first glance it looks as if we can dispose of this point by saying 'No doubt "Where did they get their authority from?" is pointless, but "Who gave them their authority?" is not'. It makes sense, too, to say 'He holds the Queen's Commission, and that is (or gives him) his authority to give orders to his Company.' But this will not bear much examination. What you are entitled to infer when I say 'I authorize you to do this' or 'Do this on my authority' is simply that I will use any force I can dispose of to support you if you do it and get into trouble. 'Authority' in this usage is part of an incantation or a threat. I cannot confer authority on you in the sense of bringing it about that people will obey you without asking questions. If I could, the lot of junior officers and assistant masters would be much less painful than it frequently is.

In quite a different way the M.C.C., the Football Association, and the R. & A. all have authority. They make and alter rules, fix and exact penalties, arrange competitions, decide conditions of entry and generally organize the playing of the games with which they are concerned in Great Britain. Their decisions are final and are obeyed. At first sight this account may seem to support the traditional use of 'authority'. A player who asked 'Why should I obey the referee?' might be answered 'Because he acts with the authority of the F.A.' But this clearly will not do. The factual information conveyed by the answer is simply that if you disobey him he will report you and then various

53

unpleasant things may happen to you, and this is talk about power and not about authority at all. The question is wrongly posed, and we can see that it is wrongly posed by asking the further question which the answer to it invites; 'And where does the F.A. get its authority from?' One might say 'From the consent of the governed' but this is unconvincing. There never was a social compact or compact of society between all footballers or between footballers as a class and the F.A. Sometimes this sort of thing occurs but it is unusual and by no means indispensable. What normally happens is something more like this.

People were playing football, cricket, and golf long before any authorities were recognized, and they played according to rules. These were not properly codified or even codified at all. They varied from place to place. And why not? Inconvenience arises only when it matters who wins (usually because money is staked on the result) or when one wants to arrange tours and away matches. So far as I know there is no controlling authority for hop scotch or (in Great Britain) rounders.

When it does become convenient to have an authority, there are several ways in which this can be achieved. The one which is most natural and most common is that the largest and best organized of the existing associations is recognized as the appropriate body to make rules for all. At the other end of the scale there is the formal meeting or Convention of those interested or their representatives. There are all sorts of variants (usurpation, intrigue, etc.) and all sorts of methods of perpetuating the authority (election, cooptation, etc.) In fact there is no one answer, though there may be several, to the question 'How do people come to exercise authority?' which is presumably what is meant by 'Where do they get their authority from?' And to say that someone has it is not merely to say that he is habitually obeyed, though that is involved.

For it is perfectly intelligible to say that a schoolmaster has lost his authority though he is still generally

obeyed because people are frightened of the probable consequences of disobedience. And it makes sense to say that a
controlling body has acted in a dictatorial, incompetent, or
dishonest way but it is still obeyed because it is practically
difficult to get rid of it and have a new one. The Old Guard
has usually quite a lot of power and some of its members at
least know how to use this intelligently to keep their jobs
even though their authority has disappeared. The linkage of
'authority' with 'power', then, is far from being fixed and
precise. It can be illustrated by examples in this way:

1. 'Al Capone is the boss here. If you don't do as he tells
   you, you will be bumped off pretty soon.' This is
   purely a statement about force so far as the general
   public are concerned. But it is quite consistent with
   the gangster's being in a position of authority in
   relation to his own group. Their account may be:
2. 'Al Capone has a good record for getting away with it,
   so you had better do what he says even though you
   don't see the point of it; and anyway he (or we) will
   shoot you if you don't.' In slightly more respectable
   circles, this develops into:
3. 'Mr Jones is an authority on economics or meteor-
   ology, so we had better do as he says, otherwise
   something unpleasant will probably happen to us
   although neither he nor anyone else will make it
   happen.'

Finally we reach:

4. 'I have every confidence in Mr Gandhi. Even though
   I do not understand his policy and nothing will
   happen to me if I oppose him, I still think it best to do
   as he says.'

Of these (1) is comparatively rare. Few people are capable
of compelling obedience without any authority even over
small groups, though there are family tyrants who are
successful at it. I am not sure that (4) ever happens; that is

to say, I am not convinced that anyone in fact does obey anyone else except (a) from habit or (b) in the belief that the other has some mobilizable force at his disposal in case of disobedience or (c) in the belief that the other is intelligent and well-intentioned and that obedience to him is therefore reasonable. These reasons for obedience do not exclude one another.

Thus it is misleading to suppose that the possession of authority adds something to the exercise of power or the employment of force. It is rather the case that force exercised or capable of being exercised with the general approval of those concerned is what is normally meant by 'authority'. It is therefore too simple to identify 'authority' with 'force rightly or justly applied.' The proper use of force is always authoritative, but authorities can be wicked and remain authoritative if most of their followers want wickedness. The career of Hitler is instructive on this point.

But however 'authority' is being used, it is true that when a number of people begin to ask in a mutinous and not a theoretical tone of voice 'Why should I obey X?' X has already lost, or is in process of losing, his authority, for his orders are not being treated as the orders of those who are correctly said to have authority are treated. Questions about the origin of authority then, in so far as they are sensible and answerable questions, are concerned with existing rights, laws, and political organization generally. They have nothing to do with magic.

§4. *'Rights'*

The wrong sort of questions about rights have the same sort of shape as those about authority with which they are closely bound up. 'How do we acquire rights?' 'Are they innate?' 'Do they entail obligations?' 'What gives a man or a government the right to impose laws?' are all the kinds of questions to which we feel there ought to be answers;

yet we do not know how to find the answers, and if answers which look feasible are propounded we do not know how to test them in order to decide whether they are correct or not. Let us begin differently and ask what it means to say that someone has a right to do something. What right has an official of the pig-marketing board to interfere with my behaviour by ordering me to fill in a lot of forms and hand over pigs I would much sooner have turned into bacon and ham for my own consumption? We have already seen that there is nothing to be gained by asking where he gets his authority from nor do we in fact mind about that. Yet we do ask 'What right has he?' and the question is significant.

The simple answer which is also the correct one is 'Because there is a law in this country to that effect.' But this, though correct, is liable to be misleading as will appear shortly. To answer the question fully, one would have to set out fully the whole complicated process by which laws are made and enforced in Great Britain and the way in which legislators themselves are elected. This would be tedious and not many people are competent to do it. Such elaborate elucidations are always boring and usually quite unnecessary. Suppose however the objector goes on to say 'Even if it is the law, I don't see why I should obey it.' The only further comment possible is 'Well, this is Great Britain, isn't it?'

The position indeed is exactly parallel to that of the cricketer who asks 'Why should I obey the umpire? What right has he to give me out?' One can answer only by expounding the rules of cricket, the position of the M.C.C., and so on. Beyond that there is nothing to be done except to say 'This is a game of cricket, isn't it?'

I believe that this is the answer and the complete answer to 'What does it mean to say that A has a right to do X?' It is however liable to look incomplete because it may be misunderstood. If the question is put in the wrong form 'What gives A the right to do X?' and if the answer is made 'the Law', it looks as if there are two things, laws and rights, of which the first somehow creates or confers the second. But this is just a piece of bad logical grammar leading to a verbal muddle. As we have seen, I have said all there is to be said about the rights of the umpire when I have expounded the rules and customs of the game of cricket and the character of the law-making body. There are not persons called 'Cricket' or 'the Laws of Cricket' which bring about a sort of biological change in other persons and make them umpires. Indeed most umpires are not appointed by anybody. Even so if we return to the inspector of the pig-marketing board it looks as if there is a doubt about him which does not arise in the case of the umpire. For I may say 'I don't think the Government has really any right to put people in that position, appoint snoopers to interfere with our private lives, give them the right of entry into our homes and so on'. Such statements are common enough in the popular press. Do they convey any information or are they simply attempts to arouse indignation against the Government? The key word is 'real' which is never simple to interpret. What does it mean to talk about 'real rights'? 'I don't believe that is a real clock' is simple enough. Perhaps it is painted on canvas as part of a stage set or has no works inside it or is some sort of practical joke. And it might be that the criticism of the Government is of that type. Possibly the law has something defective about it. There have been cases in which some oversight in legislative procedure has rendered laws invalid. If this were the case, it would clearly be proper to talk about 'real rights'. We should mean only that there are empirical tests by which we can decide whether 'A has a right to do X' is true or not. We talk about testing rights by taking the matter to the Courts.

In fact, however, this is very seldom the point at issue. What is happening is that an appeal is being made to the basic assumption that actual laws and rights are somehow reflexions or expressions of something else which stands behind and justifies them. 'They haven't really any right

. . .' suggests that there is some absolute standard by which actual legislation can be appraised and criticized. The substance of the criticism is usually that the Government, though its proceedings may be strictly constitutional, is none the less behaving in an arbitrary, incompetent, or tyrannical manner. Possibly that it is acting against the spirit or conventions of the Constitution, using its majority to pass measures for which in the modern jargon it has no electoral mandate, or depending unreasonably on delegated legislative powers.

All these are specific charges and are the kind of thing which leads to loss of authority by a governing body. If they are established, they constitute actual infringements of legal or customary rights. Nothing but confusion is caused by talking of them in the idiom of appearance and reality, since rights are not the kind of thing of which it makes sense to say that they can be either real or imitation as clocks or telephones can be. What would it mean to say that the M.C.C. has no real right to ban left-handed bowlers or forbid the sale of alcohol at Lords? Simply that if they were to do such things or try to do them, they would be asking for a revolution. So would a British Government which introduced legislation to abolish Trade Unions. But in neither case is anything gained by suggesting that real or absolute or natural rights are in question.

One further point needs attention here. It is a mistake to suppose that 'He has a right to do that' is in ordinary language a precise and definite statement. Hence it is also pointless to argue that rights exist only where codified laws exist or that codified laws depend for their validity on the existence of more primitive or fundamental moral or natural rights. To say this sort of thing is not so much false as confusing. It misdescribes the position. As we have seen when discussing authority, people do play games in accordance with rules (how else could they play them?) before the rules in accordance with which they play are codified and made precise. They behave according to rules too. We could if we liked as a piece of definition decide to use 'rights' only in circumstances where codification has already been carried out, but this would be contrary both to usage and to common sense. We do not discover rights or invent them. We formalize or codify them. But this suggests the other misconception, namely that there are (a) natural or fundamental rights *and* (b) legal rights, the second being conventional while the first are somehow necessary or part of the nature of the world.

This will not do either. Natural rights are like conventions in the sense that there is nothing logically necessary about them. They might have been otherwise, but there are usually quite good reasons for them, and codified laws are natural in the sense that they are never just arbitrary. They are formalizations not inventions. What happens when it is desired to make regulations to improve the flow of traffic in a given area? Normally observations are made to settle what most people are already doing. They are then told to go on doing it with minor modifications while the minority who have other and incompatible ideas are told to conform to the practice of the majority. It does not matter whether we say that in the earlier stage everybody had a right_1 to act in such and such a way and that a right_2 came into existence only with the new regulations, or whether we say that in the first stage there was only custom and in the second for the first time rights. What is mistaken is to suppose that either stage is more natural or fundamental than the other. Historically rights_2 are normally later than rights_1, but this is not inevitable. We can invent a new game which nobody has ever played and then rules come before customs. In this sense only can rights be invented, but the situation is not one which occurs in political development. There I think it is safe to say that rights_2 as a matter of fact always follow rights_1 and do not precede them.

If this account is accepted most if not all of the standard questions about rights are quite easily answered. What does it mean to say that animals have rights, or children, or lunatics? Either that in a particular society there are laws dealing with them, or more vaguely that all or most people disapprove of cruelty to animals, children, or lunatics. There is a further question here, namely 'What does it mean to say that there ought to be legislation or disapproval even if as a matter of fact there is not?' I shall leave this for the moment and return to it in Chapter 5.

The conclusion is that there is nothing difficult or mystifying about 'Has A a right to do X?' It is a question about political institutions and organization or a question about customs and traditions: And these are not independent questions. Except in rather unusual cases they shade into one another. Hence attempts to make 'right' a technical term and to draw a sharp distinction between legal and natural rights are misconceived. 'Right' is useful largely because it is vague. But although questions about rights are not theoretically difficult to manage, the full answers to them are nearly always highly complicated. Hence there is always a considerable temptation to embrace the illusion of absolute standards and to pretend that what is needed to answer them is not a detailed study of comparative institutions but some special insight into real, true, or absolute right. And so we get the erroneous notion of a metaphysical cupboard in which Rights, Values, and Standards generally are stored and to which only professional metaphysicians possess the key.

§5. *'Law' and 'the Rule of Law'*

Because of the interdependence of political words, a number of important points concerning the use of 'law' have already arisen incidentally in the preceding sections. We all know in general terms what 'There is a law covering that' means. Few of us can state with any accuracy what are the processes by which law is made or enforced, and for practical purposes we do not need to do so. To ask

'Why should I obey the laws of England?' is the same sort of pointless question as 'Why should I obey the laws of cricket?' It looks rather different because 'law' has had a number of different uses and has a lot of religious and semi-mystical ingredients. These need to be taken out and discarded if we are to talk at all clearly about 'law' and its relation to other political words. The chief source of trouble is a verbal confusion which tends to infect our talk about 'law' both in its scientific and in its political usage.

> Praise the Lord! for he hath spoken,
> Worlds his mighty voice obeyed.
> Laws which never shall be broken
> For their guidance he hath made.

This is a solemn and impressive pronouncement. We do not talk like that about the rules evolved by the Football Association or the Portland Club, and it is not easy to state fairly what those who formulated this and similar statements of faith had in mind. The following is I hope a fair summary of their view.

God has issued a number of commands or fiats which have to be obeyed by physical and biological creation. These are the Laws of Nature. Rivers do not choose to run downhill. They cannot help it. There is a law which never shall be broken except occasionally and by what is called a miracle, in accordance with which their behaviour is eternally and inexorably determined. The difference between these Laws of Nature and moral and political laws is that the latter can be broken since men, unlike rivers and plants, are capable of being disobedient and wicked. But still the law is there. And just as it is the function of natural philosophy to discover and tell us about natural laws so it is the function of the moral philosopher to discover and tell us about moral laws and of the philosopher of law to tell us about the true, real, or ideal laws of commonwealths.

Hardly anyone would to-day wish to defend this view in

the crude shape in which I have stated it. But traces of it in this and in more sophisticated forms still survive in discussions on law, and in questions as to the meaning of 'law' in science and in politics. In order to avoid unnecessary obscurities here, we need to be clear at the start that 'law' is used in a very different way in 'natural law' and 'political law' (or simply 'law'), and that in neither case is 'law' equivalent to 'command'.

An example will help to make this clear. (1) 'Put out that cigarette!', (2) 'Smoking in this compartment is prohibited', and (3) 'Anyone smoking in this compartment incurs a fine of 30/-' are not different ways of saying the same thing. They are however related to one another in such a way as to make it easy to confuse and conflate them. Take the differences first. 'Put out that cigarette!' is not a statement. We cannot sensibly reply 'That is not true'. 'Smoking is prohibited' is a statement about the By-laws of the Railway Company. It is like 'There is a rule against revoking' and 'You are not allowed to move your Bishop except diagonally'. In order to contradict such statements we need to show by reference to the book of rules that no such law is contained in it. An instance is Alice's reply to the King of Hearts.

'At this moment the King, who had been for some time busily writing in his note-book, called out "Silence" and read out from his book "Rule Forty-two. *All Persons more than a mile high to leave the Court.*"

Everybody looked at Alice.

"*I'm* not a mile high," said Alice.

"You are," said the King.

"Nearly two miles high," added the Queen.

"Well, I shan't go, at any rate," said Alice: "besides, that's not a regular rule: you invented it just now."

"It's the oldest rule in the book," said the King.

"Then it ought to be Number One," said Alice.'

Finally 'Anyone smoking . . . incurs a fine' is of a different type. It is a statement about what happens or tends to happen in certain prescribed circumstances. It is contradicted by 'It is quite common for people to smoke in this compartment without incurring any fine.'

Another example may help to elucidate the point. While it is true that we cannot logically contradict 'Put out your cigarette!', it is significant, though sometimes unwise, to ask for a reason for doing so. Hence we may have *A*. 'Put out your cigarette!' *B*. 'Why?' *A*. Either 'There is a rule prohibiting smoking in this room', *or* 'There is an escape of gas and if anyone smokes we shall be blown up'. Thus a command, unless it is simply of the type mentioned in the last Section 'The Boss says so' needs to be backed by a reason, and the reason may be either a rule or a law.

There are other important distinctions which the use of 'law' to cover both laws of nature and rules of conduct tends to obscure. Rules of conduct are made, not discovered. It is proper to ask of them whether they are sensible or stupid, fair or tyrannical, clear or obscure; whether they are imposed by someone or accepted from habit and custom; and so on.

But on the other side it must be noted that the distinction is not as sharp and definite as the examples chosen might suggest. Consider the following:

1. Take a dose of this now.
2. Take a dose of this before you go to bed.
3. Take a dose whenever you feel the pain.
4. A dose to be taken when the pain is acute.
5. To relieve indigestion, take –
6. Guinness is good for you!

There is a gap between (3) and (4), but (3) is not strictly a command, (4) is not exactly a rule, and (6) is not easily translatable into a scientific generalization. Thus language is not always a clear and reliable guide to tell us whether what we are talking about are commands, rules, or laws. The distinction between them is not rigid. This, however, though it is some excuse for confusion is not a defence of it.

The colours of the spectrum are continuous but we know the difference between orange and blue.

It is important to distinguish between these different uses of 'law', since endless argument and confusion have arisen because for reasons partly historical and partly theological they have been recklessly mixed up together. At bottom the trouble is the geometrical illusion already mentioned. If it is assumed that all thinking worth the name is deductive and that it starts from axioms which are not rules or prescriptions but factual truths known by recollection or by the light of nature, we inevitably conclude that natural and political philosophy are both of them like geometry (for they are serious and important studies) and that all share a common method. Thus it came about that discussions and enquiries both about the laws of nature and the laws of States proceeded on the assumption that both could be explained by employing the methods of Euclidean geometry. Only during the last century has this enterprise been finally abandoned, but it is now possible to state the situation in a more satisfactory way.

The basis of science is statistical generalization. This does not mean that axioms or calculations can be dispensed with in establishing scientific hypotheses or that they are not important. Observed frequencies can be treated intelligently and stupidly, we may have no usable hypothesis for connecting them with one another or we may be able to connect a great number of them under a wide generalization as Newton, Darwin, and Einstein have done. But however this may be they are the bed rock. This being so it makes no sense to say that natural laws can be broken. That is not because they are so terribly strong that only God is powerful enough to do it, but because statistical frequencies are not rules. They are just what happens. Hence 'miracle' in the sense of 'Divine interference with natural law' is a useless word like 'phlogiston', and to ask whether miracles happen is like asking whether phlogiston is discoverable. It is a mistake to give either a positive or a negative answer since the question is empty. We may, however, if we choose to do so, retain 'miracle' with a different meaning. Statements of natural laws are reports of observed frequencies in the world. Such reports will not cover events which are unique. When anyone maintains that he has observed such an event we do not know what to say. He may be suffering from an hallucination, but *ex hypothesi* we cannot prove that he is. 'This morning I saw my dog walking across the ceiling' would be an instance. And since such events may occur, we may find it convenient to classify them as miracles. But they would still not constitute breaches of law in the sense under discussion.

This point is important in the development of sociology, for there are plenty of laws or statistical regularities about human behaviour. There would be no associations and no rationally planned conduct otherwise. Excellent inductive arguments can be given for believing that people on the whole speak the truth, do what they say they will do, act in the way which they believe will promote their interests and so on. Politicians, admirals, and schoolmasters are all perfectly familiar with these laws; insurance companies and advertising agents have them properly worked out and formalized. Hence it is perfectly correct to say that human conduct is subject to law in the scientific sense. But we fall into a mistake as soon as we argue from this that it is in some sense determined. This is just a relapse into 'laws that never can be broken' and is a mixture of 'law' meaning 'command' and 'law' meaning 'logical' or 'deductive' necessitation. To act for a reason is not at all the same as to be constrained. Nobody has to vote Labour or Conservative in order to substantiate Dr Gallup's calculations, but his calculations may well be right in spite of that.

The laws of England however are quite a different matter. They are simply rules and their proper form is form (2) (No smoking: smoking prohibited). We know already how to connect 'law' in this sense with 'authority' and 'rights', so nothing more needs to be said about this. The only possible excuse for confusing this use of 'law' with the scientific use lies in the fact that lawgivers are normally fairly sensible and therefore avoid imposing laws (in the political sense) which can be obeyed only by a wide departure from normal or probable behaviour (law in the scientific sense). Sometimes they go wrong on this (as the legislators of the United States did with the 18th (Prohibition) Amendment) and then there is trouble. Rationing and restrictions always breed black markets. But again lawgivers do not have to act sensibly nor do they have to consider exclusively the interests of their own social group. There is a statistical probability that they will do so, but to suppose that there is any necessity in all this is simply to become confused about the logical grammar of 'law'. Euclidean geometry is necessary because it is a postulational system and not a collection of truths about matter of fact. It depends on the laws of logic, but these are laws in the sense of 'rules', not 'observed regularities'.

Finally, there is 'law' in the sense of 'command'. While it is true that many writers have said and some still say that (legal) laws are commands, I do not see how this use can be defended. The only excuse for its survival seems to lie in phrases like 'His word is law' as applied to editors and dictators; and this means simply 'His decision is final', 'There is no further Court of Appeal'.

The upshot of this discussion is that nothing but confusion follows from attempts to distinguish between 'law' and 'The Law'. There are important differences between politics and games but the function of rules in both of them is the same. There is no point in attempting to distinguish between the laws of England and the laws of croquet from this point of view. There is however a good deal to be said from a practical standpoint in favour of solemnizing the Law of the Land. Usually breaches of it are fairly important and it is a good thing to encourage people to think more carefully before they decide to break it than they normally do before infringing the by-laws of the local golf-club. But that is the only justification. No doubt it is the reason why laws have often been engraved in stone and brass, attributed to divine and semi-divine legislators and very commonly personified. Socrates in the *Crito* imagines himself talking to the Laws of Athens and being persuaded and rebuked by them, and it was once supposed that the Laws of England were not made up by legislators or judges but discovered in the same kind of way as that in which laws of nature were mistakenly supposed to be discovered. All this however is now of historical rather than philosophical interest.

But what about the Rule of Law which is commonly thought to be of great importance in democratic countries? The difficulty here is to know just what the phrase is supposed to mean. It is clear that laws do not rule except by the misleading metaphor mentioned in the last paragraph. Logically they are quite different from commands, though some writers have been misled by superficial resemblances and have supposed that they are commands. People impose laws on themselves and on other people. It is therefore odd that there should be a prevalent view that the Rule of Law is something which some people have but other people do not have, like motor cars and telephones. What does it mean then to be without the Rule of Law? Is it to have no laws at all? That is not possible.

I think the idea is really two-fold. In the first place, a judicature may be corrupt and inefficient. Access to the Courts may be difficult and costly, judicial decisions may be set aside by arbitrary decisions of the Executive, and so on. In other words a State may have a respectable legal system on paper but it may not work out in practice. In this sense it is quite easy to apply tests to decide whether the Rule of Law is maintained in a particular area or not, and it is unnecessary to demonstrate that an efficient system of administering justice is a good thing.

But this is often not at all what is meant and the second interpretation is much more dubious. By this usage '*the Rule of Law*' or sometimes '*the Supremacy of Law*' is turned into a kind of slogan or propaganda phrase. It then designates a special kind of legal system, namely one in which the type of evidence which can be produced in Court is precisely and narrowly defined and in which the accused has certain prescribed rights and privileges; in other words, not just a system of laws competently administered but the sort of system which in the United States, Britain, and elsewhere has come to be considered a satisfactory system. The reasons which can be given for saying that it is a good system are not here in question. The point is simply that '*the Rule of Law*' used in this way is a slippery term because it covertly implies approval of a particular type of legal system while purporting only to approve of the maintenance of law in general; and since the latter approval is universal (because we cannot have an association even on the scale of a village bowls club without it), the former, which is by no means universal, appears to get some sort of logical or philosophical support. Strictly speaking there is nothing difficult or impressive about 'the Rule of Law'. It is merely a convenient way of referring to the fact that associations have rules and unless those rules are pretty generally kept and enforced the association breaks down and the activity which it was designed to promote becomes impracticable. We no longer have a game of football but a general mêlée, the kind of thing that Hobbes had in mind in his much quoted description of the State of Nature.

§6. '*Freedom*'

'Authority', 'rights', and 'law' are evidently connected with one another and with 'State'. In fact if we give up supposing that 'State' stands for something peculiar and regard it simply as the word generally used to designate one type of association the other words fall into place quite easily. 'Liberty' (or 'freedom') looks rather different and it has for so long been a word used mainly to arouse emotion that it is difficult to examine it dispassionately now.

There are a number of traditional questions in political philosophy which link it with the words we have already considered. 'How can liberty be reconciled with authority?', 'Does law promote liberty or restrict it?', 'Is political freedom possible without economic freedom?'. Questions about 'will' are on the same lines. 'Is will rather than force the basis of the State?', 'Is there a General Will?', 'Does the criminal will his own execution?'.

As a preliminary to these or rather as a substitute for them it is as well to begin by asking what it means to say that a person is free. How do we contradict it? We might say 'No, he is not. He is a slave', or 'He is in prison'. But this is not very helpful. In fact, 'He is free' is an incomplete sentence. The natural challenge to it is 'Free from what?'.

At first sight it looks as if 'free from' was just an idiomatic way of stating a negative. 'He is free from want' is equivalent to 'He is not in want', 'He is free from infection' to 'He is not infected'. But this is not the whole story. 'Free from' is normally used only when an affirmative was or might reasonably have been expected. We do not say that notoriously wealthy people are free from poverty or notoriously healthy ones are free from disease. 'He is free from anxiety' usually means the same as 'He is not anxious now' (but he was till he heard from his wife or until the doctor told him it wasn't cancer). 'Free from fear' is like 'out of danger'. Both imply that something would or might have happened although it in fact did not.

We also talk commonly about 'free to . . .'. 'Smith is free to go abroad if he wants to' (there is no law to prevent him and he can pay for his ticket); 'He is free to leave the house' (he is not ill or paralysed and the door is not locked). It looks as if these can be translated into 'free from' statements without any change of meaning, but this is not the case. They are more hypothetical (if he wants to) and more positive. 'Free from' merely implies that something is not there (though it might be), 'free to' suggests that conditions for doing something are favourable (though the agent may not want to do it). In ordinary speech these uses are not rigidly separated. They tend to merge into one another. In technical discussions on politics the difference has become important. Roughly, the kind of State favoured by nine-teenth-century liberalism or *laissez-faire* capitalism was one which concentrated attention on guaranteeing its members freedom from a certain number of contingencies which had previously been inconvenient and alarming. For the most part these could be summed up as 'Freedom from arbitrary interference by executive authorities with the operation of unrestricted competition'. A certain amount of freedom to do things was also guaranteed but for most people it did not amount to very much. In fact 'free to' came to have a rather queer and unfamiliar use. It meant only 'The police will not stop you' and not as usually in ordinary language, 'You can do it if you want to'. We do not ordinarily say 'You are free to go abroad' to anyone who has obviously no money with which to buy a ticket.

To put it shortly the capitalist idea was that freedom from ... was very important and freedom to ... rather a luxury except in so far as it was a kind of freedom from ... The communist view now reverses this valuation, and capitalism in so far as it has come to accept New Deals and Welfare States has considerably changed its position. 'You are free to go to the doctor if you want to' does not in this country mean simply 'You may do so if you have enough money to pay his fee. The police will not stop you'. There is less talk of freedom from want and fear and more of freedom to work and receive a living wage. Freedom to ... is what really matters and freedom from is much less in evidence. The difference is sometimes marked by talking about the positive as distinguished from the negative State.

Now it is clear that what is at issue here is a preference for one type of political and economic organization rather than another. It makes no sense to talk about the promo-tion or restriction of freedom as such. We need to know whether freedom from ... or freedom to ... is what is being discussed: and it certainly will not do to ask 'Which of them is really Freedom?'

Indeed I am inclined to think that the whole of this distinction between positive and negative States and legislation is misleading and has propaganda rather than informative value. It tends to make the distinction between 'free from ...' and 'free to ...' far more precise and absolute than normal usage does and to suggest thereby that they are exclusive alternatives rather than complementary uses. The difference between them is real, but it has been overinflated because of the great practical importance of having legislation of the welfare type, and because of the artificial restriction of 'freedom' to 'freedom from interference' which did so much to discredit capitalism and give Marxism a good send off.

When 'freedom' is thus clarified it becomes clear that most of the traditional questions about it involve a hopeless muddle. In a trivial sense it is true that all rules restrict freedom. One would sometimes like to be allowed to make a Knight's move with a Bishop or get somebody out with a no-ball. And in an equally trivial sense, all laws promote freedom. You can safely move your Queen because the rules do not allow your opponent to make a Knight's move with his Bishop.

Those who direct their attention to the first of these trivialities tend to conclude 'There is less Freedom in England now than there was a hundred or fifty years ago, for there are more laws and regulations, that is there are more restrictions on Freedom'. Those who concentrate on the second of them say in reply 'There is more Freedom now than ever before, for there is less unrestricted and arbitrary behaviour and therefore more protection of Freedom'. These statements do not contradict one another and the apparent conflict between them is not worth discussion. They are propagandist tricks which can be made to look convincing by reference to some complicated but unimportant regulations made by the Ministry of Health or some intemperate behaviour by the village squire.

The Uses of Political Words

Nothing is gained by this sort of talk. The real point at issue is quite a different one, and is a matter of making an appraisal, or, if another term is preferred, formulating a value judgement. The question to be answered is 'What are the things about which it is important that people should be allowed or encouraged to make their own decisions?' Freedom from inspection by Government officials and freedom to go to the doctor when one feels poorly are both considered fairly important by most contemporary Englishmen. But few people seriously regard them as the only things that matter, and the importance of both of them tends to be considerably exaggerated for party political reasons.

In the same way it can be shown that 'How can Freedom and Authority be reconciled with one another?' cannot have any general answer given to it. It is part of the meaning of 'authority' that there should be rules and that these rules should be generally accepted as reasonable and kept because they are so recognized. But it is unhelpful to ask as a general question 'How many rules is it reasonable to enact?' This is an empirical question and the answer in any particular case must depend on such factors as the general standard of honesty in the population as a whole, the practical difficulties of enforcement, and generally on the gains and losses which may be expected from the attempt to enforce a particular regulation. Incidentally it should be noted that most of those who say 'I don't see why I should obey the law' are not advocating a state of anarchy. They merely want a *privilegium* to break one or two laws themselves on the understanding that other people will be law-abiding. There is not much point in being allowed to cheat at cards if your opponent is allowed to do so too.

Statements like 'Will, not force, is the basis of the State' are equally uninformative. As a general proposition this seems to mean only that most people choose to live in associations and therefore accept the conditions under which it is possible to do so. This is true but not profound. It is useful only as a corrective to the unplausible doctrine

73

that most people do not like living in associations and do so only because they are compelled.

Finally there are numerous perplexities involved in the view put forward by Rousseau that we can talk significantly about 'forcing people to be free'. We are said to do this when we compel them to do that which we rightly or wrongly believe that it is to their interest to do though they themselves do not believe this and do not want to do it. On the face of it this use of 'free' is odd and paradoxical. It is however essential to the Idealist or Hegelian system of political foundations and will be considered later. All that needs to be said of it here is that it is both confusing and dangerous.

I fear that what I have written in this and the preceding sections may give the impression that the traditional political philosophers have for the most part been wasting time by asking and attempting to answer general questions to which no answers can be given because they lack any precise meaning. To put it crudely, they have formulated questions of a type to which no empirically testable answers could be given, and such questions are nonsensical. Yet it is surely most improbable that men of great intelligence should have gone on doing this for such a long time without becoming aware of it.

Part of the answer to this objection has already been given. In the first place questions of the type which I am rejecting are the natural consequence of the early assumptions as to meaning and method which were suffered to continue uncriticized for so long; and in the second place political philosophers have not been by any means exclusively concerned with theory though the theories which are the least useful parts of their writings are what tend to predominate in the summaries of their works which are found in histories of political thought. But in addition to this the definitions they have recommended have had important practical implications of which their authors have usually been well aware and their recommendations to statesmen have frequently been shrewd and helpful. Indeed much of the difficulty we find in estimating their achievement arises because it is so hard to draw the line between their pronouncements as experts in political theory and their advice as tutors.

It is no objection to a theory to say that it is of practical importance. Indeed the opposite is the case. Confusion arises only if we go too far and, in order to emphasize the close connexion which exists between calculating and acting, pretend that there is no real difference between them. The great objection to phrases like 'Practical Reason' and 'the unity of Theory and Practice' is that they encourage us to neglect distinctions which need to be noted and emphasized.

§7. *Puzzles, Problems, and Difficulties*

Failure to appreciate the nature of the distinction between performing calculations and deciding policy is responsible for a great deal of obscurity in discussions and theories on politics. In particular it is largely responsible for the very common confusion (which can be partially cleared up by consideration of ordinary language) between puzzles, problems, and difficulties. 'Puzzle' and 'difficulty' at first sight look simple enough to distinguish from one another. A puzzle is deliberately made up and there is usually one way and only one way in which it can be solved correctly. It has always a solution and when the solution has been discovered its correctness can be checked by reconstituting the puzzle and doing it again. Hence if anyone is engaged in solving a puzzle it is always legitimate to ask 'How will he know when he has solved it successfully?' The tests vary slightly with different types of puzzle, but they can always be quite clearly and unambiguously formulated in a particular case. There is also a certifiably correct method of solving any puzzle though it is not necessarily the shortest or quickest for practical purposes. Rigorous demonstrations are often superfluous but the fact that they can be given leads us to say that there is in principle no reason why a machine should not be made which is capable of solving any puzzle correctly. In fact many puzzles constructed out of physical objects like bits of wood and pieces of wire require manual dexterity for their correct solution as well as or instead of calculation, but this does not affect the statement that 'puzzle' involves 'capacity to be solved correctly by some method or other', and where there is this capacity, a machine can be got to do the job. 'Insoluble puzzle' and 'riddle with no answer' are self-contradictory expressions.

Difficulties are quite another matter. We do not solve them (though we sometimes talk loosely about 'The solution of the difficulty'), we surmount them, reduce them, avoid them, or ignore them. There may be all sorts of ways of dealing with them and getting out of them, some of which may be more efficient than others, but there is no demonstrably correct way. Different people may have different and equally efficacious methods of coping with a particular kind of difficulty. The vicar may advise his parishioners as to their matrimonial difficulties but he cannot do their difficulties for them as he can do their crossword puzzles.

This does not mean that puzzles and difficulties have no connexion with one another. We may have no idea of how to set about solving a puzzle until someone suggests a possible method and he may do this without solving the puzzle for us. This is indeed what happens when children are taught to do sums. Or the puzzle may simply be beyond us; we may not have the intellectual or physical aptitudes required for its correct solution. Also one may say 'I am sure I could get out of this difficulty if only I could do that calculation.' There is thus a great deal of overlapping but the main distinction is clear enough. Puzzles are fabricated and have correct answers; difficulties occur and have to be surmounted. They do not have answers right or wrong, for they are not that sort of thing.

A minor point to be noted in passing is that 'difficulty'

and 'difficult' do not belong together. 'Difficult' means simply 'hard' or 'laborious'. Puzzles may perfectly well be difficult. We contradict 'This is difficult' by 'No, it is quite easy to do.' We do not contradict 'He is in a difficulty' by 'No, he is in an easiness.' It is merely an accident that we do not usually talk about 'difficult difficulties' but rather describe difficulties as 'intractable' or 'refractory'. The point is simply that some difficulties demand more thought or patience or effort to surmount than others do and puzzles differ from one another in the same way. But the distinction between difficulties and puzzles is not of this kind.

'Problem' as it is commonly used is vague and slightly confusing since it is equivalent sometimes to 'puzzle' and sometimes to 'difficulty'. There are chess problems and bridge problems, but also unemployment problems and Negro problems. To use the same word in all these is to run a serious risk of practical error. Possibly it happens because 'problem' sounds less trivial than 'puzzle' and more intellectual and theoretical than 'difficulty'. It suggests too what is perfectly true, namely that we do habitually make use of calculations to help ourselves out of difficulties. But it also suggests what is false, namely that ability to solve puzzles is the sole or the primary qualification for dealing with difficulties. As Aristotle pointedly observed, schoolboys are often very good at doing arithmetic and geometry; they are not equally adept in the field of morals. It is well known that a boy may have a high I.Q. and be quite unfit to act as secretary to the School Cricket XI. It would be a pity however if 'problem' were discarded since there are situations which occur and which we need a word other than 'puzzle' and 'difficulty' to describe. Puzzles are fabricated and have pre-determined solutions; difficulties occur of themselves and may be dealt with in various ways, none of which can correctly be described as 'right'. There are however some situations which occur without our deliberately making them up and in which it does seem appropriate to talk about 'the right method' and 'the right answer'. Thus Bridge experts sometimes say 'Here is a problem which occurred in actual play', that is, the distribution of cards was not planned, it just happened; but the result is just as if it had been planned. We can treat it as a puzzle and solve it.

This situation is still partly fictitious since the number, design, and method of distributing the cards are all predetermined, and so are the legitimate moves that can be made with them. But there are plenty of completely natural situations in which the same procedure is permissible. The most notorious are those concerned with the behaviour of solid bodies in motion, and in particular the behaviour of the planets. Newton might perfectly well have said 'This problem arises in actual play', that is 'It is just as if someone had fabricated the planets deliberately so that their movements could be predicted by solving geometrical puzzles.' This indicates the reason why the existence of problems as distinct both from puzzles and from difficulties has been frequently overlooked. If we accept the anthropomorphic conception of a God who has constructed the universe in the sort of way in which a jig-saw puzzle or a bridge puzzle is constructed, then what we call our difficulties in living in it and finding out about its workings arise only because it is a large puzzle and therefore difficult for our immature minds to solve. But since it is a puzzle there must be a correct method of solving it, and Descartes for instance believed that he had discovered that method; other great mathematicians have slipped into the same mistake.

But we have no method of knowing *a priori* which parts of nature will present us with problems. Inanimate material objects certainly do so, and so up to a point do living bodies; human beings to put it mildly are much less reliable. There is however no reason why any matter of fact should provide us with problems unless we are prepared to say that we know that electrons or cells are, for these purposes, just like playing cards. Yet the only way in which we could begin to find this out (if it is true) would be by showing empirically that our calculations about them give fairly reliable predictions.

Now it is eminently reasonable that in political matters we should hope to find problems, that is, questions which have definite answers, which will assist us in dealing with our difficulties; and that we should then make use of our ability to make and solve puzzles in order to get the answers to our problems. Thus the frequent occurrence of mass unemployment under a capitalist system was a difficulty which threatened to wreck the system. Nobody could suggest any method of overcoming or escaping from it. Keynes maintained that it was a problem which could be solved and replaced it by a set of mathematical puzzles. This is a considerable over-simplification, but it is intended only as an illustration of the kind of process I am trying to clarify. In fact we commonly make use of exactly the same procedure in ordinary life in planning a journey from A to B or in deciding how many rolls of wallpaper we need in order to cover the walls of the dining-room. Engineers solve puzzles in order to build bridges and General Staffs solve them when planning invasions or ordering aircraft to carry atomic bombs.

What tends to be forgotten is that this process is not always legitimate or helpful and that it never by itself surmounts any political difficulty whatever. It is not surprising that this should be overlooked because of the immense range of subjects in which this kind of substitution has been found empirically to work with a very high degree of efficiency. We forget now what a long time it took before people came to realize how difficulties concerning pumps, bridges, and steam engines could be efficiently replaced by puzzles to which competent mathematicians could produce the right answers. But although we now know, because men of genius have found out for us, that some natural phenomena present us with problems and that these can be answered by solving well-chosen puzzles, we certainly do not know that all or most political difficulties belong to that class. No doubt it looks as if they ought to do so, especially if we start by assuming that human associations are for all important purposes just like planetary systems or even like ant-heaps, and a great deal of political theorizing has clearly proceeded on these lines. It may be admitted that the puzzle solving which we do in arithmetic and geometry may not be perfectly appropriate in this department, but it is also taken for granted that there must be some axioms rather like those of geometry and arithmetic from which we could deduce the answers to political puzzles and apply the answers to political difficulties.

There are two dangers inherent in this procedure. In the first place, as we have already observed, the applicability even of Euclidean geometry to matter of fact is something which has to be decided empirically. It is true that some of the difficulties we meet with when we try to measure material objects can be overcome or eliminated when we know how to make use of geometrical and trigonometrical methods. But the pseudo-axioms of politics ('The State is by nature prior to the individual'; 'All men are created equal') have neither the lucidity nor the *prima facie* applicability which the axioms of Euclid have. There are indeed some problems of a political character, that is, concerned with the behaviour of people in associations, which we know how to deal with and which help to mitigate our difficulties. A good deal, for instance, is now known about disease, nutrition, and industrial organization. Here we are clearly in the region of problems. They are not set by anybody, but they have answers. Incidentally, the answers are seldom of the simple 'Yes' or 'No' variety, nor are they usually expressible by simple numbers. One may say 'A great difficulty which we must try to cope with is the prevalence of a particular disease, but we are well on the way to solving the problem of inoculating the population against it'. If the question is put 'And how will you know when you have solved it?' the answer is usually not 'When nobody has the disease any more' but 'when the incidence of it is reduced below *n* per cent of the population'.

We cannot set any *a priori* limit to the area of human relationships which can ultimately be dealt with in this way, and it seems clear to some optimistic scientists that all our difficulties will some day be reduced to trivial dimensions by the progressive formulation of appropriate problems which can be solved by puzzle-solving techniques. I doubt whether this view is correct because I do not see any reason to suppose, or indeed any meaning in saying, that the world has been fabricated or created; hence there is no ground at all for holding that it has been so constructed that all difficulties can be overcome or eliminated by scientific research. But this is not a question on which discussion can profitably take place since no definite sense can be given to it. What is clear at the moment is that many of our most pressing political difficulties are not expressible as problems in the sense in which I am using 'problem'. No doubt the difficulties in the way of international co-operation would be greatly reduced or even eliminated if human beings were different from what they are. But what problem are we supposed to solve in order to deal with the situation as it is now?

This brings us to the second danger which springs from the over-simplified doctrine that clever puzzle-solving is a panacea for political difficulties. The position of the statesman and that of the engineer are not analogous. If the engineer finds that facts are refractory and prevent his puzzle-solving from getting him out of his difficulty, he may change them forcibly if he can. Sometimes objections are raised on aesthetic grounds, but generally speaking if he wants to fell trees or divert the courses of rivers to facilitate his bridge-building there is no objection to his doing so. If his puzzle-solving does not fit the environment he has to decide whether to alter the environment, or set himself a difficult and more complicated puzzle, or admit that the difficulties in his way are insuperable in the circumstances. Some would perhaps maintain that this is precisely the position of the statesman; and if animals are regarded as complicated machines and human beings as complicated animals there is no objection in this case either. There is however no reason to believe that this is so; indeed to say that it is so is demonstrably false. It is for these reasons that the confusion between puzzles, problems, and difficulties which tends to infect political theory cannot be dismissed as a harmless eccentricity and that phrases like 'social engineering' are to be regarded as something of a menace. Economic planning is rather like engineering in that both proceed from difficulties to problems and from problems to puzzle-solving. Provided that this is done consciously and the limitations of it are recognized (as they are, for instance, by Professor Popper in his advocacy of 'piecemeal' as distinct from 'utopian' engineering) there is much to be said for it. Unfortunately, however, matters do not always stop there. If theoretical puzzle-solving fails to deal with difficulties because of refractory human behaviour there is always a temptation to do what the engineer does to the scenery rather than to admit that the puzzle-solving was inappropriate or was on the wrong lines. If the Jews or the kulaks are or appear to be the obstacle, one can liquidate them in the hope that when they are out of the way the theory will work after all.

This is one side of the general intellectualist fallacy about political organization which will be considered in detail in the next Chapter. At this stage, however, I should make it clear that the alternative to intellectualism is not anti-intellectualism. Hitler was not the first to notice that clever puzzle-solving is not the only qualification for dealing with difficulties. His mistake was in supposing that it was not a qualification at all. He saw rightly that ruling was not a technical skill, but supposed mistakenly that he had no need to acquire or make use of technical expertise but could rely safely on his '*schlafwandlerische Sicherheit*'. With luck this sometimes works, so does action which appears to be derived solely from deductions from political axioms. But neither is reliable.

CHAPTER 4

Political Foundations

§1. *Foundations in general*

I AM not sure how the subjects discussed in this Chapter should be described. The popular term nowadays is 'ideologies' but this is ugly and unhelpful. 'Foundations' is not much better but I cannot improve on it. I do not myself think that democracy or communism have foundations in any significant sense. But they are popularly supposed to have them. By this I mean that the types of political organization called 'democracy', 'fascism', and 'communism' are usually said to rest on, or to be the expression of, distinct political philosophies or ideologies.

This sounds curious. From the time of Herodotus men have argued as to whether monarchy, oligarchy, or democracy was the best form of government, but this is an entirely different question. One may quite well consider now whether the advantages of having a constitutional, hereditary monarch are greater than those of having a popularly elected President as Head of the State, and it is by now obvious as it could hardly be to the Greeks of the fourth century B.C. that there is no general answer to this. Sparta, Athens, and Thebes were at least sufficiently alike to make it a reasonable assumption that what was best in the way of a constitution for one of them would do pretty well for the others. The same sort of questions can be asked about Oxford and Cambridge Universities. Their constitutions differ a good deal in detail but their functions and difficulties are so similar that divergences in principle would be rather surprising. But the differences between Britain and the United States are in many ways more striking than their resemblances.

Plato has nothing to say about divergent ideologies in the

modern sense. For him there is the ideal *Politeia*, of which tyranny, oligarchy, and democracy (in the Greek sense) are more or less imperfect copies. Hobbes, Locke, and Rousseau do not talk the language of ideologies. They could have done so without much difficulty, but in fact they assume that there are good and bad States and they do not argue about bases or foundations. It is only with Hegel and Marx that this sort of difference becomes explicit and even with them and their successors it is far from easy to decide exactly what it is that the argument is about. One feels the same difficulty with the moralists of the nineteenth and early twentieth centuries. Mill, and Sidgwick, and Bradley, and Croce, all of them openly and sincerely believed that they were disagreeing with one another over something factual and important. They were disagreeing about the foundations of morals. Yet just what it means to say 'A and B are disagreeing about the foundations of morals', or 'of politics' is not immediately apparent.

Suppose we are looking at the dog of our hostess. I say 'Fluffy is a Peke', and you reply 'No, he is an Aberdeen'. We know what we are disagreeing about and how to settle the issue. If I say 'The Athens of Pericles was a democracy', and you reply 'No, it was an oligarchy' the matter is rather more complicated because of the vague and conflicting uses of 'democracy' and 'oligarchy'. But if we agree on usages and find out enough about Periclean Athens there is no room for argument.

Modern political arguments over foundations are not like that. It is true that Mr Dean Acheson and Stalin both wanted to claim a sort of proprietary right to the word 'democracy' rather as if it were the name of a patent medicine. But that was not the essence of their disagreement and they did not for a moment suppose that it was; nor were they reviving the Herodotean dispute on monarchy, oligarchy, and democracy. In fact, they agreed with one another on this far more nearly than either of them agreed with the British or the Dutch or the Belgians.

Anyway it is now almost universally held that monarchy, oligarchy, and democracy in this practical sense are matters of expediency rather than of principle.

What then are these foundations or principles which are so important and the subject of so much disagreement? And how, if at all, are they connected with practical political organization? I have already suggested that they are closely connected with axioms and postulational systems. For this reason too they have many points of resemblance with competing systems of dogmatic theology where it is often equally difficult after a particular controversy has died down to say with any confidence what point of substance was at issue between the disputants. Essentially the search for foundations is a search for proofs and much of the trouble about morals and politics has arisen because this search has been undertaken without any prior enquiry as to what it means to talk about proofs in this sort of subject.

I shall now examine the three great systems of political foundations, but before doing so it may be helpful to say a little about terminology. For purposes of this discussion 'democracy', 'capitalism', and 'liberalism' are alternative names for the same thing. This is not to deny that there are important differences between the capitalist system as it works with comparatively little adulteration in the United States and the social-democratic Welfare State which has been created in Great Britain. It means only that there are certain describable characteristics concerned with electoral methods, representative government, the rights of the individual in the Courts, the freedom of the Press from Government control, and the virtual absence of Government interference with religious teaching which are found in varying degrees in the United States and Western Europe and which are not found in the U.S.S.R., China, and most of Eastern and Central Europe. This usage steals 'democracy' back from the communists, but there is no help for this. Common usage in Western Europe and the United States is the decisive factor. One can say 'capitalist democracies' and 'communist' or 'new democracies', but this only promotes confusion. Some would further claim that Welfare States on the British model constitute or will soon constitute a new intermediate type, and that our classification should be 'Capitalist democracies' and 'Socialist democracies' opposed to 'Communist States'. This is purely a matter of convenience, as will become clear in what follows. In the same way, States whose alleged intellectual foundations are Hegelian idealism are often called 'Fascist'. This is a confusing usage since it is largely accidental that this nebulous ideology has been so closely connected in recent experience with the Third Reich of Hitler and the Italy of Mussolini. 'Capitalist', 'Socialist', and 'Communist' all have descriptive uses. 'Fascist' is only a vague word of abuse.

§2. *Democratic foundations*

Modern democratic theory differs from the theories of idealism and communism in that there is no one man of genius to whom the formulation of it can be attributed. Admittedly Hegel and Marx derived much from their predecessors and contemporaries as any thinker of importance is bound to do. But it is beyond dispute that each of them was responsible for a political theory which stands to-day pretty much where its creator left it. There have been important modifications in detail but that is all. Democratic theory is in a different position. There is no one book or author to whom one can turn for the classical exposition of it. Locke's *Second Treatise* or Mill on *Liberty* are obvious candidates, but neither has the breadth of vision or the depth of insight that the *Rechtsphilosophie* or *Kapital* exhibit. They are brilliant essays, not great works. In fact it looks at first sight as if the preachers of democracy had not gone in much for foundations. This, if true, might well be to their credit. But I do not think it is the case that they wrote and spoke as they did because they saw clearly that the search for foundations was a futile one. They seem rather to have taken the line that their foundations unlike those of metaphysical speculators were obvious or self-evident. Jefferson did not think he was saying anything new or startling in the Declaration of Independence. He thought that George III knew as well as he did that all men were created equal and endowed with natural rights. But George III was wicked or misguided and would not admit it. By contrast neither Hegel nor Marx supposed for a moment that what he was saying was already known to all intelligent men.

Actually democratic theory in its modern form has two patron saints, one of them involuntary and the other deliberate. They are Sir Isaac Newton and Immanuel Kant, and the link between them is Jean Jacques Rousseau. This may sound rather a surprising trinity to select, but I think the choice can be justified. The key is given by Kant himself in a well-known passage in which he explains his debt to Rousseau. Newton, he says, had demonstrated that the movements of the heavenly bodies were not arbitrary but proceeded in accordance with simple and regular laws. Rousseau had done the same for human societies. There is nothing mysterious about States any more than there is about the solar system. They are just assemblages of common, individual men held together by law. We have seen already that this use of 'law' is confused and misleading, and up to a point Kant realized this too. But if we allow ourselves to use this kind of language, democracy does need to have a metaphysical foundation of some sort.

That this is the case becomes clear as soon as we ask what the force is which holds men together in society in the way in which gravitational force holds the planets together in the solar system. This again is a badly posed question, but whatever Newton himself may have thought, many of his followers unquestionably believed that gravitational force was the name of a sort of invisible string which prevented bodies from flying apart. The picture thus presented of the physical universe seems to-day a very queer one. But in enlightened circles in the eighteenth century it seemed strange and almost impious to question it. 'God said, "Let Newton be" and all was light.' Berkeley and Hume from slightly different points of view were extremely sceptical as to its efficacy but neither had any usable alternative to put forward. The laws of Newtonian mechanics were not seriously challenged for another century.

What then were the invisible strings which held society together? An answer was easily forthcoming. 'The desire which every man feels to promote his own interest'. This was plausible enough, especially when the accepted psychology took it for granted that 'desire' and 'aversion' stood for internal pulls and pushes. Indeed 'attraction' and 'repulsion' are themselves psychological terms used metaphorically in descriptions of physical phenomena.

In the first instance these usages were too vague to occasion any serious confusion. It was the achievement of the political economists to give precision to them and thereby to provide a kind of Newtonian psychological foundation for much political thinking in the eighteenth and nineteenth centuries. For by making suitable definitions and solving some simple mathematical puzzles it is possible to demonstrate that when every man pursues his own best interest he thereby tends to raise the standard of living enjoyed by all. This doctrine was indeed parodied in a somewhat unfriendly way by Mandeville in his *Fable of the Bees*,

> Thus every part was full of vice,
> Yet the whole mass a Paradise;
> Flattered in peace and feared in wars,
> They were the esteem of foreigners,
> And lavish of the wealth and lives,
> The balance of all other hives.
> Such were the blessings of that State;
> Their crimes conspired to make them great.

On the other hand many moralists including Bishop Butler subscribed to it with some reservations. It was therefore eminently respectable. As Marx unkindly pointed out, it was likely to be so since it made thrift or greed the only important virtue and therefore encouraged the pioneers of capitalism to do as a duty exactly what they proposed to do in any case. But, as is the way with puzzle solutions, it left some tiresome difficulties to be faced. In the first place it was fairly obvious that the masses did not know (since they were not learned in the works of the economists) where their own interests lay. This could be overcome by education or more simply, as we know now, by providing Government Departments with highly trained Public Relations Officers. The second and more formidable difficulty was that even when everything had been clearly explained to them they might still not choose to act as cool self-love dictated. Particular passions and affections were always liable to interfere. And finally and worst of all it had to be admitted that except possibly in the very long run (by which time all or most of them would be dead) the steps required to benefit the State as a whole would not be beneficial to the people who had to take them. Saving for posterity does not raise the standard of living of the savers. Hence something more difficult than self-interest in the obvious sense had to be invoked to provide the bond by which it was assumed that the State must be held together.

There was another side to this picture in which Rousseau and others were more interested than they were in the doctrines of the economists. It is roughly what is meant by the phrase 'the Rights of Man'. Here again the Newtonian system is very much involved, but in a rather different way. For what is in question is not the glue which holds the State together but the arbitrary character of despotic rule. Not unnaturally, the French and the American middle classes in the eighteenth century felt much more strongly about this than the English did.

I do not mean to suggest that thinkers who lived before the seventeenth century were not puzzled about States and about natural rights. We have already seen that they were.

But the remodelling of the fundamental Greek assumptions to fit Newtonian theory was a drastic one and it ensured that no important question would look quite as it had done before. Regularity, predictability, and above all manufacturability, since the Newtonian world was first and foremost a superb machine, were now the prime intellectual requirements. It was the whims of monarchs even more than their cruelty which made them odious to the intelligentsia. This yearning for certainty is at least partly to blame for the rather strange redefinition of 'freedom' and therefore of 'rights' which becomes prominent at this time.

The much quoted opening statement of Rousseau's *Social Contract* provides the best clue to the whole system. 'Man is born free; yet everywhere he is in chains.' The idea is that men are born with rights in the same way that they are born with arms and legs. They are deprived of the enjoyment of these rights by the arbitrary actions of monarchs just as they may be deprived of the use of their limbs by fetters. Now it is an essential ingredient in the standard mechanistic theory of the universe that universal causality does not in itself restrict freedom. This has to be maintained if 'freedom' is to be kept in the vocabulary at all, and there are overwhelming commonsense and theological reasons for doing that. So 'freedom' is redefined, explicitly by Spinoza and implicitly by Rousseau and many others, as 'recognition of necessity'. We are worried by our sufferings because we believe that they might be alleviated if we knew how to do it. Restraint is irksome as long as we think that it need not happen. But it is nonsensical to repine about what is inevitable. We may not like a wet week-end, but it is unreasonable to complain about it unless we mean to say 'I might have known it was going to rain if I had listened to the weather forecast'. If we did listen and the forecast was right we have nothing to grumble about, for we knew what was going to happen. We chose to go away on a week-end that was going to be wet and it would therefore be ridiculous to call the foreseen weather a restriction of our freedom. Of course we do not at present have accurate foreknowledge of physical phenomena and to that extent it is correct to say that we are not free. But the cure for this is a more efficient meteorological office. Ignorance is servitude, knowledge of necessity is freedom.

The application of this to politics is easy enough. Provided that laws are clear, simple, and rigidly enforced, and provided they do not arbitrarily prevent us from taking the most advantageous course of action which natural necessity leaves open to us, we are free. Otherwise we are in chains. Hence the puzzle of politics can be readily stated and Rousseau had no difficulty in stating it. It is to find a form of association in which everyone is absolutely bound by law and yet obeys only himself and is therefore as free as he would be if no association existed. He is free in the redefined sense of being permitted by law to do what it is in his best interest to do; he knows or can easily discover the inevitable consequences of his possible lines of conduct. Thus the economic and the political arguments reinforce one another. What we need is simply a collection of intelli‹ gent human beings held together by political laws which ensure their freedom from all arbitrarily imposed restrictions. Economic laws are laws of nature in the old, discredited sense and when once they are known they no more restrict freedom than the law of gravity does. They control our administration just as gravity controls our movements, and there is no harm in that. Let the (arbitrary) government of men be replaced by the (rational) administration of things and all will be well. So Rousseau believed, and greater intellects than his have since echoed his faith.

But the difficulty is still there. Who is going to make and enforce the admirable laws by which States are to be regulated? Here Rousseau began to fumble. It would be comforting to say 'Intelligent men will recognize that such laws are needed. They will be unanimously agreed by a Convention or Assembly and enforced by officers appointed in the same way'. But that was too much even for

Rousseau's optimistic belief in the essential soundness of the common man, and his final view which involves a semi-divine legislator or Führer and the forcing of recalcitrants to be free is not at all democratic in the Western sense. It leads on to Stalin and not to John Stuart Mill.

It is at this point that foundations seem to be required. For it is hopeless to define 'rights' and 'freedom' either in terms of 'what everybody wants to do' or of 'what everybody would want to do if each was perfectly intelligent and aware of all the causal sequences in nature'. In Kant's language, all that we extract from this is a collection of hypothetical imperatives. 'Do A if you want B.' 'If you want to promote the general happiness, you must take steps to ensure full employment.' Hence some categorical foundation was needed. 'You ought to act so as to promote the general happiness whether you want to or not.'

In this Kant was partly right and partly wrong. He was right in maintaining that current theories did not do what they claimed to do. They did not provide any bridge leading from natural laws to moral and political laws. Hume put the point more clearly when he pointed out that 'ought' cannot be logically derived from 'is'. Neither the fact that most people want a shorter working week nor the fact that they might have it if certain legislation were enacted nor both of these facts together provide any logical demonstration that such legislation ought to be passed.

To prove this sort of conclusion we should need another premise of a different kind, namely one which itself contains an 'ought'. Where Kant went wrong was in supposing that such a premise might be discovered and that it was an important part of his job as a philosopher to look for it. His belief in the possibility of a metaphysic of politics was a mistaken one, since the difference between factual and normative statements is not of the kind which he supposed that it was.

But Kant and those of his successors who shared his mistake did the only thing they could do. They looked for the foundations of democracy in the one direction which offered even the prospect of success, namely in the direction of the inalienable rights of man. The doctrine now becomes something like this. 'Empirically man is not free and no political devices can conceal or evade this fact. But in a more important transcendental sense, he is free. He ought to be free in the empirical sense too, but this freedom cannot be achieved under the conditions of our existence on earth. We can only approximate to it. All we can say is that man has a natural right to be treated always as an end in himself and never merely as a means to something else, and this does follow logically from the idea of him as a transcendental person, though not from the idea of him as an empirical or natural phenomenon.'

Precisely what this means cannot be briefly or simply elucidated. The crucial point about it for our purposes is that it is and claims to be a metaphysical view and, as such, to be beyond the range of empirical confirmation. The argument is that we cannot infer the existence of inalienable rights or deduce categorical statements about duties from any statements about matter of fact; and this is correct if the meaning of 'statements about matter of fact' is restricted as empiricists have frequently restricted it to 'observations of the most simple and elementary kind'. And since we certainly do want to talk about rights, and since (as the illusion of absolute standards encourages us to believe is the case) we cannot do this significantly unless we are acquainted with absolute or inalienable rights, it looks as if we are committed to believing and if possible demonstrating that all men do have such rights; and this demonstration must be *a priori*, that is of the geometrical, nonempirical variety. It is at this point that the 'Faculty of Reason' begins to play an important part in the story.

I do not propose to dwell here on the errors of faculty psychology. They have been demolished too often to deserve any further attack. It is enough to point out that one of the worst of them is the doctrine that 'Reason' is the name of a sort of tool or implement with which we think and not simply a descriptive word for referring to one group of our intelligent activities. This mistaken doctrine however has been widely followed from early times and has led to the illusion that men have Reason in the same way that they have eyes and ears. When, therefore, it is said that the possession of Reason is what distinguishes men from animals, it is not immediately obvious that what is meant is simply 'All or most men can talk to one another intelligently. They can use marks and noises as symbols. There is no evidence for saying that any other animals can do this except possibly in a very rudimentary way. In other words, talk about Reason is just talk about a special competence which human beings acquire fairly readily and which, as far as we know, is peculiar to them.' On the contrary, Reason is treated as the name of a very precious possession and it is easy to argue that it is because and only because they possess it that human beings are entitled to be treated with a special kind of respect. Kant and many others have thought that if an animal did possess it (and the test is that it can talk intelligently in the first person singular – use 'I' correctly) it would be entitled to the same respect, that is, would be endowed with natural rights. Thus Rights come to be founded on Reason, and Democracy appears as the only type of constitution appropriate to Rational Beings.

This argument that human beings ought to be treated as ends in themselves, that is, ought not to be treated arbitrarily as things or instruments, because they are the posssessors of Reason, is one side of the metaphysical foundation of democracy. The other side which is closely bound up with it is that of the State as founded on an original or basic compact, the Compact of Society. The belief that the rules of associations are binding on their members in virtue of a compact or promise is at least as old as Plato and, as we have already seen, it has some force in that governing bodies are sometimes set up as a result of explicit agreement between people or associations (like the Federal Governments of

Switzerland and the United States) and they continue to exercise authority only so long as they are recognized by their constituents as authoritative.

But what contract theories of government normally assert is much more precise and much less plausible than this. It is that all governments depend for their authority solely on an original compact which binds not merely those who make it but their successors in perpetuity. Clearly this will not do at all. The Pilgrim Fathers actually put their names to a Compact of Society before landing in New England. It had commercial rather than political significance and it is not the foundation of the laws of the State of Massachusetts. For suppose that the whole of this story of a compact were proved to be a myth invented by pious posterity. Does anyone suppose that the force of the laws of Massachusetts would be thereby destroyed or weakened? What if the signatures to the Constitution of the United States were conclusively proved to be forgeries? That would be a point of great historical interest but no political consequences would follow from it. In fact the notion of an original compact is worthless. Yet as long as people assume that 'Why should I obey the law of the land?' is a sensible question, they are reluctant to abandon the notion of a compact altogether. And so there is a tendency to substitute a metaphysical compact for a historical one.

Here again the notion of Reason comes into play. It looks as if we can properly ask 'What sort of laws does Reason demand that men should enact for their own government?' and this is just another form of 'What would be the rules of a perfect or ideal association?' Now the Law of Reason is logic. Hence it seems fair to say that the laws which perfectly reasonable beings would adopt would be universal, equally binding on all, and would never lead to contradictions. From this it is not difficult to see how Kant came to his categorical imperative 'I ought never to act except in such a way that I can also will that my maxim should become a universal law.'

Political Foundations

The metaphysical foundations of democracy then are roughly these: (1) human beings as such ought to be respected because they are endowed with Reason; (2) they are bound only by laws of their own making, and to be bound by such laws is to be free; (3) Reason provides them with a test by which they can satisfy themselves of the appropriateness or otherwise of proposed or actual laws; (4) the test is whether these laws would be acceptable to a community of completely rational beings. I do not suggest that democratic writers and thinkers have all been as metaphysical as that, but I believe that their proofs will not work unless these or very similar premises are accepted.

What we really want to know however is what is the use of all this. Suppose we could accept the premises and the reasonings, should we be any better off? I think that we should not. The objection to this sort of argument is not merely that it depends for its force on the fallacious assumptions considered in Chapter 2, but that the conclusions to which it leads are either vacuous or highly disputable and not at all self-evident. The position is not that the statements which go to make up the fundamental principles of democracy are false or that the basic rules of democratic legislation are bad. It is that we are mistaken in supposing that what we have to do with here are statements or rules at all. Admittedly 'All men are created free and equal' looks like a statement and 'Men are always to be treated as ends and never as means' looks like the formulation of a rule. It is natural to suppose therefore that we have here fundamental rules from which others can be deduced. If this were so 'foundations' would be a suitable word for describing them. But it is not so. Nothing follows from these high abstractions, or if you like anything does. They are not concerned with actual people but with 'real' or metaphysical ones. By themselves they tell us nothing whatever about how to deal with prisoners of war, criminals, or taxi-drivers. We can derive no actual law from them and appraise no actual law by means of them. That is what I mean by saying that as foundations they are useless. They do not and cannot do what they purport to do, that is, serve as axioms from which practical conclusions can be derived.

Their function is quite a different one. They are much more like the model Bye-Laws which are issued by the Home Office to guide subordinate legislative bodies, or like forms which require to be filled in before they give any information. It is easy to see that this is in fact the way in which they work. Take for example the well-known clause in the XIVth Amendment to the Constitution of the United States, 'nor shall any State deprive any person of life, liberty, or property, without due process of law, nor deny to any person within its jurisdiction the equal protection of its laws'. This looks like, and is often taken as being, the statement of a fundamental democratic principle. But what exactly does it mean? As it stands the answer is 'Nothing'. It is a formula which has no application until the variables which it contains are replaced by actual values. We do not even know what kind of values it will accept. When it was passed nobody supposed that it protected legal persons as well as actual ones. It was not intended to make the world safe for big corporations nor need it have done so. But the Supreme Court ruled that it did, i.e., that the names of corporations could be used to fill one of the blanks.

So these basic principles do not, as their formulators hoped they would, make arbitrariness impossible. They simply transfer it from the monarch to whatever body is empowered to interpret them. And 'interpret' means 'decide how the blanks can be filled in'. There are not two types of law, namely fundamental law and derived or positive law, of which the second is a copy, reflexion, or expression of the first. The mistake which is made by those who have supposed that there are may be illustrated in this way.

There are rules of Association Football, Rugby Football,

Northern League, American Football, Seven-a-side, and perhaps of other kinds of football as well. It would be possible to take all these and construct a sort of schema or form which would cover all of them if the blanks in it were suitably filled up. One might even verbalize the result, though it would be rather awkward to do, and say 'Football is played by two sides, each consisting of a specified number of players on a field of limited dimensions' and so on. The result might be described as the fundamental rules of football, but this would not be a happy description, since you could not discover the laws of any actual game by reasoning from it. You would however gain some information about the use of the word 'football', and be able to say with confidence when taken to watch a game of cricket 'They are not playing football'. That is about as much as can be done with the fundamental principles of democracy. A great many very dubious proceedings can easily be reconciled with them by means of suitable definitions. But there does come a point at which one can say with considerable confidence 'I don't think *that* régime could be described as democratic in the ordinary meaning of the term'.

It must be repeated however that by no means all writers about democracy have made this mistake. Many have recognized that it is right to obey the law on nearly all occasions and wrong to torture people in concentration camps. And they have avoided asking the further and mistaken questions 'Why is it wrong?', 'What makes it wrong?' It is only when these questions are asked and no straightforward factual answers to them are discoverable that the plunge into democratic metaphysics is taken and found in the end to be of no assistance. It is pointless to invent an axiom that men ought always to be treated as ends in themselves in order to demonstrate the truth of 'It was wicked to send people to Belsen or Buchenwald', for this is not the sort of statement which requires or admits of demonstration.

Yet when all is said and done it may fairly be claimed that the metaphysics of democracy unlike those of the rival ideologies has done a great deal more good than harm. Although it proves nothing, the belief that it does prove something has at least tended to encourage humane rather than brutal conduct. It is true that human beings are very important, but they are not important because they are possessed of Reason or because God created them or because of anything else. 'Because' is out of place in this context. The chief reason why philosophers have tried so hard to insert it is that they have been alarmed by a demon called 'Subjectivism' and have sought to exorcise it in this way; but as I shall show in Chapter 5, this demon is illusory, and if he were not he could not be disposed of by any metaphysical argument about foundations. Unfortunately the alternative foundations of politics which will now be considered, though they are theoretically as valueless, have been practically far more deleterious than any variety of the democratic mythology has ever been.

It may be said that these criticisms of democratic foundations are out of date. They are relevant to the theories of the eighteenth and early nineteenth centuries, but nobody nowadays talks about the rights of man or the supremacy of Reason. In modern terminology the foundations of democracy are representative government, universal suffrage, social equality, and, of course, the Rule of Law. The precise meaning of such claims as this is not very clear. They may perhaps be regarded as the formulation of tests by which we can decide whether the term 'democracy' is being correctly used or not, and if this is the case they are only of linguistic interest. But if more than this is meant, the arguments already advanced against the earlier statements of democratic foundations still apply to them. They are either vacuous or, if they are made specific by being given a definite context (England or the U.S.S.R. in 1953), their rationality or advisability is a matter of discussion and controversy in which empirical arguments are highly relevant.

There is then nothing sacrosanct about them and it is inappropriate to describe them as foundations.

§3. *Hegelian foundations*

Hegel disagreed violently with all the ideas which we considered in the last section. He did not believe that Newtonian physics was the whole truth about nature, he did not hold with the equality of man or universal brotherhood, he did not regard perpetual peace to be the ideal which politicians should try to achieve, and he did not recognize the type of State which capitalist economy was bringing into existence as the last word in political organization. There is therefore a quite legitimate sense in which he can be described as a reactionary against the Enlightenment of the seventeenth and eighteenth centuries. But it is a most misleading over-simplification to represent him as one who believed that all the achievements of those centuries were worthless shams which should be discarded in favour of a return to the political feudalism and Aristotelian science of the Middle Ages. He believed as Marx did after him that feudalism and capitalism were both defective because they were one-sided. Capitalism, or, as he called it, Civil Society, was merely a denial of feudalism or family organization. Once it had happened, however, you could not just discard it and go back, you had to go forward and evolve something different in which the positive elements in feudalism and capitalism were both preserved. It was here that Marx disagreed with him. The Marxist case against Hegel is that Hegel's third stage or synthesis is really a pretence and a sham. Hegel did want to return to the pre-enlightenment era of politics, but found it inexpedient to say so. Hence he produced a pompous and mystifying system to disguise his true purpose.

It cannot be denied that this view is plausible. Hegel himself said a number of things which are detestable about the divinity of the State and the purifying and ennobling

character of war. He did profess to regard the Prussian
State of the early nineteenth century as the highest type of
political organization, and his doctrines or what purport to
be his doctrines have been said to provide the foundation
of many totalitarian and reactionary systems of government.

One must not overlook all this, but it is a mistake to make
too much of it. It is as unfair to blame Hegel without
further enquiry for the atrocities of the Third Reich as it
would be to saddle Jefferson or Locke with the responsibility for the excesses of the French Revolution. And this is
perhaps the best point from which to start in trying to
interpret Hegel sympathetically. Like Burke he was
obsessed by the horrors of the Revolution, and also like
Burke he did regard them as being the inevitable product of
the metaphysical foundations of democracy. But at this
point Burke and Hegel part company. Burke hated all
metaphysical abstractions. Hence he attacked the British
Government for quibbling with the Americans about verbal
niceties like 'sovereignty' and 'virtual representation'
instead of taking sensible steps to remove their genuine
grievances and reach a practical settlement; and he
attacked the French revolutionaries for overthrowing the
traditional institutions of their country in the service of
abstract propositions concerning the social contract and the
rights of man. 'Civil Freedom,' he said, 'is not, as many
people have attempted to persuade you, a thing that lies
hid in the depth of abstruse science. It is a blessing and a
benefit, not an abstract speculation; and all the just reasoning that can be upon it, is of so coarse a texture, as perfectly
to suit the ordinary capacities of those who are to enjoy and
those who are to defend it. Far from any resemblance to
those propositions in geometry and metaphysics, which
admit no medium but must be true or false in all their
latitude; social and civil freedom, like all other things in
common life, are variously mixed and modified, enjoyed in
very different degrees, and shaped into an infinite diversity

of forms, according to the temper and circumstances of every community.'

Burke and Hegel both hated democratic equalitarianism in practice and both wanted to reduce its practical efficacy by demolishing its metaphysical foundations. Burke, however, wanted to achieve this by convincing his hearers that all metaphysical foundations were rotten because they were metaphysical; Hegel sought to replace what he held to be the defective metaphysical foundations of democracy by the superior ones of his own system. Not less but more and better metaphysics was his remedy.

What then was the defect of the metaphysics of the Enlightenment which needed to be cured? In Hegelian language this metaphysics was defective because it was abstract. Newtonian physics was abstract because it conceived the 'real' world, the world behind observable phenomena, as consisting of a vast number of distinct independent atoms held together by invisible strings called 'causes' and 'forces'. Democratic political theory was abstract because it conceived all human associations as similar collections of atomic persons held together by the invisible strings called 'contract' and 'interest'. But these abstractions were not in Hegel's view to be regarded as primary. They were not the opening moves in the metaphysical game. They were inevitable counter-moves to another set of one-sided abstractions which had preceded them. In his technical language they were the antithesis to an earlier thesis, the negation of an earlier affirmation. This earlier view was the medieval conception, or what Hegel took to be the medieval conception, of the world as a single whole or lump of Reality of which the parts were just appearances or aspects or manifestations. This is not helpful or even significant language, but I do not think that the vague idea which it is trying to formulate admits of any clear statement. One can only talk in analogies and say that for the natural philosophers of the Middle Ages what mattered was Creation as a whole. The details of secondary causes were relatively trivial and unimportant. For Galileo and his successors, what mattered were the individual parts and particular causal laws. The notion of an underlying whole was neglected. This up to a point is true and important, though the distinction is a good deal less precise and clear than Hegel wanted to make it.

The position as regards political organization is considerably easier to formulate intelligibly. It may not be true but at least it makes sense to say that the actual basic unit of primitive human associations is the family. Tribes, nations, and so on are for practical purposes indistinguishable from large families. And in this sort of association it is status, not contract, that matters. The metaphysic of this is the rudimentary organic theory expounded in the legend of Menenius Agrippa and many other early writers including Plato. It is that what is real or important is solely the association. It makes no sense to say that individuals have rights against it any more than it would make sense to say that the parts of the body have rights against the body as a whole, and nobody claims that a poisoned limb has a right not to be amputated.

In fact this is not at all typical of medieval political theory but is a much earlier and more primitive view. But it is convenient to pretend that it was typical and some extreme statements which support such a belief could easily be produced. What is true is that the importance of the individual as an actual factor in political affairs (and not simply as an immortal soul) was very much greater in the seventeenth and eighteenth centuries than it had been some centuries earlier.

But Hegel's criticism of earlier metaphysical systems has something in it which is important. When he calls them abstract, he does not merely mean that they are incomplete. He condemns them on the ground that they set up their own incomplete stories as accounts of something behind and beyond what is actual, that is, as Reality. This is fair criticism and in making it Hegel was stating a vital part of the truth. Indeed, as contrasted with both neo-Platonists and mechanists, he was as much an enemy of metaphysics as anybody. But it is his positive contribution which is in question here and which is much less happy. For having decided that absolute things, rights, laws, and so on, will not do since they are empty hypostatisations of abstract definitions, he still believes that metaphysics is in principle possible. Certainly there is no other world lurking behind this one and represented by it. But there is a structure inherent in this actual world which philosophy can discover and elucidate. Strictly speaking 'structure' is wrong. One of the main troubles about the old systems was that the Reality which they purported to describe was static and this was itself a symptom of their abstract character. The structure which Hegel believed himself to have discovered was dynamic; it was a rhythm which could be discovered in anything actual and he called it 'the Dialectic'.

Now although the distinction between Reality and Appearance as the older philosophies had described it was altogether wrongly drawn (since there is no 'beyond' with which the actual can be contrasted), Hegel did not want to discard it. He redefined it on Aristotelian rather than Platonic lines. 'Real' for him became equivalent to 'concrete', to 'what a thing is capable of becoming', much as Aristotle had thought of the nature of a thing or person or institution as being what it was potentially or what it would be when fully developed. In different and more modern terminology Aristotle and Hegel were both insisting that 'That is not a real State' was equivalent to something like 'That is not properly developed, but it would be a State in the strict sense if it were properly developed'.

The crucial point in Hegel and the doctrine by which he fully recognizes that his system stands or falls is that of the Dialectic. It is too difficult to be made intelligible in a sentence or two but it has played such an alarming part in the history of political thought in the nineteenth and twentieth centuries that something, however brief, has to be said about it. What it is supposed to do is to provide an *a priori* or necessary ingredient in the process mentioned in the last paragraph. It is the immanent metaphysic of change or development. More simply one might say that at the beginning of the nineteenth century it was coming to be recognized that the biological as well as the physical sciences were interesting and important, and it was at least not at all obvious that the Newtonian model would be the right one to use in developing them. Kant for one was convinced that it would not be. The notion of ' *L'homme machine*' was already discredited and it was becoming clear that if there was to be a metaphysical structure of reality at all it would have to be one in which change, growth, and development were explained and not explained away. The Hegelian explanation is however a very queer one and I hope to show that when it is examined it is really not an explanation at all. Briefly it is that 'X grows' or 'X changes' or 'X develops into Y' are equivalent to 'For X (thesis) there is substituted not-X (antithesis), and then for X and not-X there is substituted Y (synthesis) which incorporates both X and not-X in itself'. Put differently, the affirmation which is the thesis is confronted by the denial which is the antithesis, and the contradiction between them is itself negated in the synthesis.

Stated crudely in this way the system looks like mere verbiage. What can it mean to say that being is negated by not-being and that the contradiction between them is negated by becoming? We can observe bodies like billiard balls collide with one another, but it is mere confusion to use the language of negation or contradiction to describe what happens. And in what conceivable sense can it be said that an institution such as slavery negates or contradicts anything? It seems a trivial and obvious misuse of language to talk in this manner.

Although there is a lot more that can be said on this issue and in spite of the fact that many serious writers have claimed and still claim that there is much more in the dialectic than this, I believe that in the end there is nothing to it. Hegel's statement of it is difficult to deal with because he systematically confuses statements about language with statements about matter of fact and irretrievably muddles up logical with psychological and biological arguments; he also uses a cumbersome and high-sounding terminology which has a mystifying effect; and finally much of the persuasiveness of his central theme, the Dialectic, is derived from a simple ambiguity of the German word '*aufheben*'. This word has three main uses: (1) to lift up; (2) to preserve; (3) to cancel. All these are combined in the transition to synthesis or negation of negation. No similarly ambiguous word exists in English, and therefore Hegel's expositors are driven to coin neologisms like 'sublate' in order to translate his most important word. This in itself suggests very strongly that confusion and not clarification is generated by Hegel's own use of it.

It is indeed noticeable that dialectical explanations have never had much popularity in the advanced sciences. Except at a very elementary and popular level their defects are so manifest in physics and in chemistry that they lack even initial plausibility. In the biological sciences in spite of some heroic efforts by able controversialists the position is not any better. We give no factual information by saying that the growth of plants is or involves the negation of negation. But in the backward sociological sciences (including at least a good deal of psychology) the position has been different, and it is not hard to understand why this should have been the case.

As we have seen, the demand for foundations in politics was of very long standing. Allegiance to the State is an important matter and therefore it seemed proper to ask for some basis or justification for it of a different type from that which was required in the case of subordinate associations. Attempts to provide such a basis by exploiting the notions of natural right, contract, and the rule of law were not successful.

and the ideas of divine right, inherited authority, and arbitrary power in general were equally discredited. On the face of it what Hegel had to offer had a lot to be said for it. In the first place he claimed to provide a proof. It was difficult to follow and therefore difficult to refute conclusively, but at least it purported to demonstrate that loyalty and obedience to the State were rational and indispensable to civilized human beings. The State itself too was given a solid foundation in Reason. It was not just an accidental association but the necessary result of something rather impressive and mysterious called the Dialectic of History. In obeying it you ranged yourself firmly on what was bound to be the winning side, which is always a satisfactory thing to do. And finally, for those who did not want to understand the intricacies of the dialectical method itself, the version of history which it was supposed to validate was in many ways acceptable, especially to Hegel's fellow countrymen. There is a lot of good and obvious empirical evidence for what is called the swing of the pendulum in politics. An overdose of absolutism does tend to be followed by a period of democratic reaction and vice versa. The Greeks knew that extreme democracy often begets tyranny.

Of course Hegel meant much more than that. He was not trying to develop an empirical theory of individual and crowd psychology. But many of his adherents have been impressed by the fact that at least some successions of events do fit in well enough with the metaphysical theory which he elaborated. It is not surprising that this should be so since the occurrence of a dialectical rhythm in nature is not asserted as a scientific hypothesis which can be confirmed or refuted by observing facts. It is supposed to be necessary or *a priori* and therefore can no more be confirmed or refuted by observation than the conclusions of Euclid can be; that is part of what is meant by calling it 'metaphysical'. Nor is it supposed to be just a consequence of the way in which language is constructed. 'There is a dialectic of history' and 'All events manifest a dialectical process' are supposed to state facts about the world which are neither purely logical nor purely scientific but somehow incorporate both logical and scientific validity. It is important to recognize that this claim has to be made if the Dialectic is to fulfil its purpose and provide a metaphysical foundation for politics.

It is worth mentioning here that all philosophies of history are in the same position in this respect. By accumulating a great deal of historical information one can make them look like empirical hypotheses which are strongly confirmed by observational evidence, but that is not what is intended. It is part of the meaning of 'the philosophy of history' that something more than ordinary inductive evidence can be obtained as to the origin, growth, and decline of cultures and civilizations. For the number available for comparative study of a scientific kind is much too small to justify the formulation of anything but very tentative guesses about their behaviour. Hence in practice the 'laws' in accordance with which they are supposed to rise and fall are always empty hypotheses. They cannot be confirmed or refuted by any facts independent of those which they are invented to explain, and therefore the explanation they purport to give is a sham. It is conceivable that regularities sufficiently marked and specific to make reliable prediction possible may some day be discovered in this department, but at present words like 'civilization' are used far too vaguely for anything of the sort to be attempted with the slightest prospect of success.

But even this very qualified optimism is out of place where Hegel's dialectic is concerned. In spite of his claim that he has corrected the abstractness of his predecessors and unveiled an actual process immanent in nature and not a bare 'beyond' or 'other world', the Dialectic cannot be considered as anything but a purely metaphysical invention. For how could the assertion that politics or history or any other process develops dialectically conceivably be proved or disproved? What is the antithesis (in the ordinary not the Hegelian sense) which might be true but in fact is

false to the statement that all development is the negation
of negation? I shall have more to say on this point in connexion with the Marxist development of Hegel's view.
It is enough to point out here that Hegel's supposed foundation of politics is completely useless. It is not false but it is
vacuous.

For what in the end is Hegel asserting about his concrete
State? Nothing, I think, except that it satisfies the condition
formulated by Rousseau that in a genuine State everyone is
completely bound by law and yet obeys only himself and is
therefore as free as he was before. We may well agree with
Hegel that neither the family nor Civil Society satisfy
this requirement, and also that they fall short of it in
different ways. But what we want to know is the practical
method of avoiding this difficulty. What are the actual
institutions and legal arrangements by which the Concrete
State or Ethical Society does the trick? And about this we
get no enlightenment whatever either from Hegel himself or
from his successors.

This is not accidental. It follows from the way in which
the law of dialectical development is formulated that anybody except an ultra-philosophical radical can accept
Hegel as his authority either for maintaining or for changing
the *status quo* of any association to which he happens to
belong, and almost any practical political policy can be
given a Hegelian endorsement. Hegel himself used his
doctrine to support Prussian absolutism and glorify wars of
aggression. Bradley and Bosanquet held that it would under-
write what we should now call a liberal or a moderate conservative line. Others again press it into the service of the
British Labour Party's conception of the welfare state, and
it should be remembered that in Italy Croce as well as
Gentile took Hegel as his master.

It is easy and rather tempting to suggest that by saying
this we present Hegel with a testimonial. There must surely
be something very profound about a philosophy which such
different types of politician can accept. Even Burke, it may

be said, could have found in Hegel the philosophical foundation for his belief in custom and tradition rather than abstract speculation as the rock on which ordered society is founded, and Marx's debt to Hegel is not in question. All this is further evidence for the universality of Hegel's genius and of the truth of the dialectical principle which he discovered.

This kind of defence entirely misunderstands the point at issue. For the fact that the dialectical movement is held to be omnipresent and all-pervasive is precisely what reveals its emptiness and futility. It is just an instance of the kind of illusion which non-empirical or metaphysical thinking about matter of fact always generates. The uselessness of it may be shown thus: suppose I say 'Everything that happens, happens in accordance with the will of an omnipotent Demon', and you reply, 'Where is he? I don't see him'. I say 'You can't see him or observe him in any way'. 'Then I suppose you know he exists because ordinary causal explanations are somehow defective. What you mean is that we should give up bothering about them and try to find out what the will of the Demon is?' 'No. Causal explanations are sound as far as they go. Causes are what the Demon wills.' 'Well, then, suppose the Demon ceased to exist, but causal explanations went on working as they do now, would any detectable difference be made in the observable world? Could we in fact know that the Demon had perished?' The conclusion of this is obvious. 'Demon' in this sense is a useless word like 'phlogiston'. Statements like 'The Demon wills it' give us no new information about anything. Exactly the same is true of 'the dialectical process'. Because it is said to control everything it is completely useless as an explanation of anything in particular. It is logically futile because there is no antithesis with which it can be contrasted.

It may be said that this is a trivial objection. It is a demand of human reason that our knowledge should be unified, and the notion of universal dialectical development should be regarded as a great unifying concept and not as an extra piece of knowledge. This assertion, however, is itself worthless because it uses 'unification' in an empty and meaningless fashion. A unifying hypothesis is one which connects a number of other hypotheses and enables new theories about matter of fact to be framed and tested experimentally. Thus Newton's hypothesis connected those of Kepler and Galileo and gave rise to a large number of further hypotheses which could themselves be confirmed or refuted. But the Dialectic is not at all like that. It is not even claimed that the theory of the concrete State replaces those of the family or Civil Society in this kind of way.

I have dwelt at some length on this aspect of Hegel for this reason. Most of his successors and he himself when he talks practical politics make no use of the dialectical foundation except a purely verbal one. It has no use. They adopt instead a simplification of the view which is practically indistinguishable from the old-fashioned organic theory of the State. But if the latter conception is criticized, Hegelians claim with apparent justification that this is unfair to Hegel since he held a different and more difficult view. What I have argued is that the strict Hegelian doctrine in so far as it is different from the cruder versions commonly attributed to Hegel is vacuous as the foundation of any political policy. We must now consider the simplified version which is not empty but is mistaken and deleterious.

Briefly, it is that the names of States are the names of persons of a very special kind. It is not a metaphor to say 'The United States are pacific', 'The U.S.S.R. is aggressive'. Such statements are literally true or false in the same sense that 'Smith is pacific', 'Jones is aggressive' are true or false. In the same way it makes literal and not metaphorical sense to speak of States and perhaps of other types of association as being endowed with will, intelligence, courage and so on. From this it is reasonable to infer that States have their interests to promote and dangers to avoid. If then we go on to ask about the rights and duties of Smith and Jones the answer seems easy. These are determined wholly and completely by the interests of the State, for it is contrary both to common sense and to common usage to talk of the members of a person having rights against the person whose members they are. This does not pretend to be a metaphysical theory or foundation at all. In fact it is one in so far as it claims anything but *de facto* validity. There is nothing but a linguistic point in the statement 'The parts must (or must not) be subordinate to the whole of which they are parts'. Beyond this there is only an analogy which is not really a very strong one between the relation of the parts of the human body to the body as a whole and the relation of members to the associations of which they are members. The argument and the analogy have been employed by persons of great weight and literary genius, but they do nothing to demonstrate that associations are persons against whom their members have no rights.

But in so far as this type of argument has frequently been put as a justification or a foundation for reactionary political programmes it is important to ask whether it can be convincingly disproved or not. For it may not be demonstrable as its more ambitious exponents have held that it was, but it may still be right.

The best analysis of it, of which the following is a summary, is that contained in Mr J. D. Mabbott's book, *The State and the Citizen*. The idea that the names of associations are names of persons arises from a simple linguistic muddle which can easily be exposed. 'Russia is aggressive' is grammatically just like 'Jones is aggressive', but the logical grammar of 'Russia' is very different from that of 'Jones'. In simple cases this needs no further argument. 'Russia went to the polls last week' is clearly a statement about Molotov, Vishinsky, Ivan Ivanovich and the rest of them. So is 'Russia is aggressive'. The factual information it conveys is information about the actual and probable behaviour of individuals. This might equally well be given (though it would take a long time to do it) by factual statements about individuals in which the word 'Russia' never occurred. Thus 'Russia' is shown to refer not to a person but to a logical construction.

Next we have statements referring to the legal and economic relationships in which associations stand to their members and to one another. These are slightly more complicated but their analysis presents no serious obstacle. The key to it is provided by what has already been said about words like 'own' and 'owe'. It is a linguistic convenience to pretend that 'the State', 'the Corporation', or 'the College' are names of persons who can own property, pay rents, collect bills and so on. Hardly anyone however is misled by this fiction except where the State as distinct from other kinds of association is involved. It is not our practice to personify the L.C.C. or the N.U.R. or to conceive them as persons who pay grants or cash cheques. We are well aware (until we puzzle ourselves deliberately) that statements which refer to them are actually statements about chairmen, secretaries, treasurers, and other officials.

We can deal in much the same way with psychological statements in which the names of associations appear as subjects. Thus 'England loves Queen Victoria' is recognized without difficulty as a statement about the sentiments of all or nearly all the inhabitants of England. So are 'England trusts Sir Winston Churchill' and 'England respects President Eisenhower'.

A more serious difficulty is found in statements where the name of the association occurs not as the subject but as the object of a psychological attitude. It is words like 'patriotism' and 'loyalty' which are the strength of the simplified Hegelian case and which the opponents of it find most awkward to explain satisfactorily. How about 'Sir Winston Churchill loves England'? Unquestionably this does give information about Sir Winston Churchill's actual and probable behaviour in many specifiable situations. But is that all? Could not the behaviour be as it is but the statement still be false? He might conceivably be pretending but doing it so cleverly as to deceive the world. That, however, is not the point. What we want to know is whether the statement 'Sir Winston Churchill loves England' can be translated without change of meaning into a different statement in which 'England' does not occur but is replaced by a large number of statements about specific happenings, scenes and customs which Sir Winston Churchill enjoys and approves.

Probably most people will feel that this analysis is incomplete. Whether we are talking about England or the N.U.R. or the local cricket club, loyalty, devotion, and patriotism at least seem to involve more than tendencies to act in certain ways. If a man does not pay his subscription and is not prepared to suffer any personal inconvenience in the interests of the association, we deny that he is loyal to it and are not convinced by his protests that he is deeply moved by its economic or political plight. Yet when he does behave correctly, it still seems proper to ask 'Is he *really* loyal?', 'Does he *really* care at all about the fortunes of his country or his union?' And this leads us to wonder again whether there is not something in the view that associations are after all persons though of a rather odd kind. To this Mr Mabbott has two complementary answers. In the first place he points out that 'fear', 'love', and 'hate' are more complicated than they seem to be. 'Fear, love, and hate are feelings which ought to have objects but sometimes have none. "Jones fears ghosts" means that Jones believes that certain noises etc. are caused by certain disembodied yet localized spirits, and Jones is afraid. The fear would be reasonable if the belief were true and the objects existed . . . A patriot's illusions about national greatness and national honour . . . also centre around realities – the honour of his government and the welfare of its individual subjects. But his illusion creates no further object other than land and men, and land is no object of devotion'.

In the second place, to fill the void which he admits that this analysis will leave for many readers, he claims that loyalty is a legitimate sentiment if it is directed or felt not towards England but towards 'certain ideals of life and government', that is, towards what is sometimes now called, though Mr Mabbott does not use the phrase, 'the British or the democratic way of life'. Unquestionably these are good reasons for being sceptical as to the soundness of all claims that States or other associations are persons or super-persons except in a strictly metaphorical sense. But it would be misleading to say that we have here a logical dis-proof of all such claims. To urge this would be to give to logical analysis the wrong sort of testimonial. It can never prove or disprove the existence of anything, and this inability is not like the inability of an aged motor car to get over the Simplon Pass; it is like the inability of any motor car to write a poem or compose a symphony.

This point is important and requires further elucidation. Take first the case of Jones' fear of ghosts. There are pos-sible experiences, like those attributed to Hamlet and Macbeth, which, if they were authenticated, would entitle Jones to say 'Now you see I was right after all. You were able to explain away my churchyard sights and haunted house noises, but you cannot get rid of this one – so perhaps I was right about the others too'. This however will not stand up for long. An apparition of John Bull or Uncle Sam or even Athene is not the kind of new evidence we want to assure us that 'Britain', 'the U.S.A.', and 'Athens' are the names of real persons. In fact we cannot say what sort of new evidence there might be which would be relevant in this context.

This, however, is awkward but perhaps not fatal. For consider Epicurus and the early atomists. What evidence did they want to show that atoms were genuine entities and not just fictions based on a weak analogy from motes which can in favourable circumstances be seen by the naked eye? 'Very tiny particles' will not do since it soon comes up against the standard objections, 'Are they coloured, or smelly, or even heavy or hard?' In fact the only evidence which would have established their case was evidence which they not only could not get but could not even remotely envisage, namely tracks on photographic plates in a Wilson chamber.

This line of argument will not bear investigation, but consideration of it shows more clearly why organic theories of the State or of any other type of association are not susceptible of either proof or refutation. What the early atomists were doing was to produce an hypothesis to explain certain observable and puzzling facts. They had no means of verifying this hypothesis, so it would be better to describe it as a happy guess, but they were right in claiming that the facts demanded an explanation and that atoms would provide one. The position as regards associations is quite different. As we have already seen they do not need any explaining. When their character is analysed the reasons for creating them and for obeying their rules are not obscure or puzzling. We may if we like describe them as persons, though it is rather misleading and may be politically dangerous to do so, but no factual point is at issue here. Hence we should not claim to refute or disprove the claim of anyone who chooses to use language in this way. It is indeed no more surprising that we should feel affection for the Old Country or the Grand Old Party than it is that we should feel it for the Old Home or the favourite animal. No supernatural entities in the background are needed to explain any of these sentiments; nor, if it is contended on other grounds that such entities (whether personal or not) exist, does their existence contribute anything to our knowledge of anything factual. The claim of Hegelians to provide foundations for political obligation needs no refutation since it dissolves as soon as it is carefully examined.

§4. *Marxist foundations*

Marx preached revolution and the revolution he wanted was a genuine one. It was not at all the gradual reconstruction that appealed to Fabians or Social Democrats and it was entirely different from what has been described as the Social Revolution that has occurred in England in the last ten years. 'Revolution' in Marxism is fairly strictly defined. It does not mean vaguely 'any substantial change in existing social and economic relations', it means 'the annihilation of a ruling class'. What is involved is a cataclysm, not a gradual change. It is this and this only which has enabled it to replace Christianity as the gospel of the oppressed wherever they exist in Western countries and to penetrate to great areas in Asia and Africa where Christianity has never gained anything more than a tentative and precarious footing.

Many people find this truth unpalatable, but it is necessary to recognize it and to appreciate the force of it if we are to understand the strength and the weakness of the Communist position. Official Christianity has always with some qualifications stood for the maintenance of the established political and social order; and the most important qualifications have concerned the right to remove or to disobey rulers hostile to the Church. As far as the poor were concerned they were poor either as a result of their own vice or incompetence or as a consequence of Original Sin. Poverty was inevitable and in part a good thing since it provided scope for the Christian virtue of charity. In any case poverty was a trivial matter since it affected only this life and was therefore dust in the balance compared with the rewards and penalties of Heaven and Hell. This did not mean that the Church was always opposed to social reform. It did and does mean that revolution as a means of achieving such reform was excluded.

What Marx said was quite simple. Poverty is unnecessary. It is not the result of the Will of God but of special economic and political conditions. It can be got rid of by changing those conditions, but the present ruling class will never make the change because it is not to their interest to do so. Hence there must be a revolution. And what is more, the revolution is bound to be successful because the industrial revolution has produced conditions in which the poor are bound to win. Therefore they need not wait as Christianity advises them to do for posthumous happiness. They can be happy and free from poverty here on earth, but only if the existing ruling class is wiped out.

It is as well to state the view thus crudely to start with since unless this is done rational criticism of it tends to be overwhelmed by torrents of misrepresentation and righteous wrath. When the dynamic appeal of it is once seen, it is no longer surprising that it should be regarded as devilish and untouchable in some quarters and should be watered down by politicians of a different hue who want to exploit its appeal to the oppressed without accepting its revolutionary implications. That is why it is necessary to treat its foundations rather differently from those of democracy and Hegelianism. Roughly most people know the policies which these are supposed to support, though as we have seen they are incapable of supporting anything. But whereas a good deal is known about the actual workings of political and economic institutions in England, the U.S.A., Hitler's Germany, and Mussolini's Italy, the same cannot be said about the U.S.S.R. The fact that this is mostly the fault of the Russians makes no difference.

In this case, then, we have two matters to discuss. The first is the empirical argument to which Communism can appeal and the second is the metaphysical foundation on which it claims to rely for its ultimate justification. It is extremely difficult to distinguish between these in reading the works of Marxist writers, because Marx and his successors have an unhappy tendency to emphasize the latter, which is spurious, and to play down the former, which is often cogent.

Marx believed that sociology was a science, that is to say, he held that the behaviour of human beings in States and other associations was capable of being explained and predicted, and the key to such explanation and prediction was

given by knowledge of the conditions of economic production. It is an observable fact that the political organization, laws, and culture of any society are controlled by those
who control the means of producing food and other
material commodities. In an agricultural community what
matters is the ownership of the land; in an industrial community it is the ownership of the coal, the iron, the factories,
and the capital resources generally. Hence if we want to
predict the behaviour of a community, what we have to
discover is (1) who control the means of production, (2)
what course of action by the community do all or most
of those who control the means of production believe
will conduce to the expansion of their own material
wealth.

In this form what is offered is a straightforward hypothesis about communities which can be verified in the
ordinary way. Nothing whatever needs to be said about
determinism, moral or religious motives, or indeed about
motives at all. The central argument may be put like this.
'If you want a reliable forecast as to the behaviour of any
group of people under specified circumstances, find out
what are their economic interests. They will frequently give
non-economic reasons for what they propose to do. They
will advance moral, religious, and cultural justifications for
it. You need not worry about these. Your best bet is to
consider solely the probable economic consequences to
them of the proposed course of action.'

There is nothing revolutionary or even very surprising
about this. It is simply a statement about observable
regularities. It is statistically verifiable and has long been
the basis of calculation most commonly employed by
practical politicians. Indeed there is nothing at all shocking
in the statement that we can estimate fairly accurately the
extent and bitterness of the opposition which may be
expected to any project of reform by finding out whose
economic position will be adversely affected if that project
is carried out. Such a statement may well be criticized on

the ground that it is not sufficiently precise for purposes of accurate prediction, but there is no point in attacking it as cynical, and anyone can easily satisfy himself by reference to the daily papers that it is roughly true. Marx did not discover it. Aristotle, Machiavelli, Hobbes, and Adam Smith had all of them taken it for granted. What Marx did was to convert it from a vague to a fairly precise statement by concentrating attention on the means of production, for this gave his answer to the question, 'Why are the rich rich and the poor poor?' The rich are rich because they control the means of production, the poor are poor because they do not. There is nothing mysterious or divinely ordained about it and the mechanics of the process are easily explained. If the poor are going to survive at all they must have access to the means of producing food, clothes, and other material commodities. It is economically advantageous to the owners of the means of production, that is, of the capital resources of the community, to permit the poor to use them under the least favourable economic conditions which the poor can be compelled by the threat of starvation to accept; and therefore the poor are inexorably pressed down to the point at which they are paid for their labour just enough to keep them alive and enable them to produce more workers to replace themselves.

Hence we may construct a further hypothesis to the effect that in every society there will be a class of owners who exploit and a class of labourers who are exploited. 'Exploit' means simply 'pay as little as they can for labour and use the threat of starvation to get as much as possible out of it without considering anything but the way in which to get the maximum of private profit'. Again this is a perfectly factual statement, and the statistical evidence in favour of it in England in the middle of the nineteenth century was formidable. It was assembled by Engels in *The Condition of the Working Class in England in 1848* and by Marx and Engels in *Capital*.

Assuming then that capitalist exploitation of labour was

inductively established as a general sociological law it was possible to frame and verify further hypotheses. One could see why the booms and slumps which happened periodically in capitalist countries took place, why there was generally a mass of unemployed, why colonial expansion was needed, and why there were recurrent wars. Other important conclusions such as that the workers in capitalist countries would certainly suffer a continued fall in their standard of living, and that middle classes would tend to disappear, have not worked well, but subordinate hypotheses can be framed to accommodate them.

If it is accepted that reliable predictions are possible by this sort of method, the argument for revolution is easy. There are strong empirical grounds for asserting that no ruling class ever voluntarily surrenders its privileges and powers. But there are similar grounds for maintaining that under modern conditions of production the position of the ruling capitalist class tends to get steadily weaker. It is weakened by recurrent crises and wars which it has not any method of avoiding, while the workers are progressively strengthened by the spread of literacy and in particular by the increasing realization that their poverty is not inevitable. If they choose their opportunity they can overthrow the rulers, assume power themselves, and use the means of production to raise their own standard of living instead of increasing the profits of the present owners. The essential point is to choose the right moment which may be expected to occur during or immediately after a war (there are many good empirical reasons in favour of the latter), and it is the job of sociological experts to know when the circumstances are most favourable, that is to take advantage of a revolutionary situation when it occurs.

What happens next is more nebulous. There is far less empirical evidence on which to base reliable predictions. But it may be expected on general psychological grounds that the dispossessed owners will try very hard to upset the new régime and that they will be helped by the ruling classes in countries where no revolution has occurred. There will be counter-revolutionary movements which have to be suppressed. So there will have to be a period, indefinitely long, in which strong government will be required. This is the dictatorship of the proletariat. The workers are now organized as the ruling class to defend the revolution and repress all attempts to reverse it. Finally and still more nebulous there is the classless society in which the government of men is replaced by the administration of things and repression is no longer necessary. There was nothing very novel in most of this argument. Marx himself wrote, and Lenin quoted him in *The State and Revolution*, 'The honour does not belong to me for having discovered the existence either of classes in modern society or of the struggle between the classes. Bourgeois historians a long time before me expounded the historical development of this struggle, and bourgeois economists the economic anatomy of classes. What was new on my part was to prove (1) that the existence of classes is connected only with certain historical struggles which arise out of the development of production; (2) that class struggle necessarily leads to the dictatorship of the proletariat; (3) that this dictatorship is itself only a transition to the abolition of all classes and to a classless society', (1852).

What the Marxist programme does is rather to force into prominence a political factor which democrats and Hegelians had either ignored or kept in the background. Both had generally admitted that as a matter of fact some existing States at any rate were not very satisfactory. Both however had tacitly assumed that nothing much could be done to alter this in the short run and had taken it for granted that with the increase of enlightenment or rational behaviour things would get progressively better, though they had different ideas about what 'getting better' meant. Marx contradicted both of them on this point by producing empirical reasons for expecting things to get progressively worse and by asserting bluntly that nothing but a series of violent revolutions could be plausibly expected to produce a form of association in which it was genuinely the case that everyone obeyed the law and yet in doing so obeyed only himself and remained as free as he had been before.

This situation indeed could not be reached immediately (as far as could be seen). There was the intervening period of dictatorship to be gone through. So what Marx was saying to the workers was something like this. 'You can achieve freedom from poverty and unemployment if you choose, but there is a price to be paid. You must sacrifice at least temporarily some "Freedom to . . ." In your case, however, this does not amount to much. You are not now free to dine at the Ritz or go for holidays abroad. You have nothing to lose but your chains and you have the world to gain.'

It is perilous to say that this was or is a weak argument. A great deal of very sound evidence can be produced to support every move in it, and even the concluding stages are by no means wild and unsubstantiated guesses. But as I have stated it, it is an empirical argument which might always be refuted by further investigations into observable facts. It is a sociological hypothesis and not a statement of revealed truth. Thus it would be relevant to urge against it that things have changed a good deal since 1848. It is no longer a safe guess in Western Europe that employers will sweat their workers or that they could do so if they wanted to. Organized labour is a powerful force and has extracted substantial political concessions. Democratic political institutions which may or may not have been the complete sham that Marx said they were when he wrote about them have at least a great deal of weight behind them in some countries now. And, most important of all, ways have been found of mitigating, perhaps of escaping from, the booms, slumps, and heavy unemployment of the nineteenth and early twentieth centuries.

Hence it is quite arguable that the Communist statement of the situation even when it was elaborated was only a good first approximation to the political and economic organization of capitalist society and that it is no longer even that. This would not be very surprising. Marx was a pioneer, and except for the faithful Engels he had no followers of any great ability during his life. His own acquaintance with political and economic organization even in England was very indirect. He had read much but observed little of what went on in British commercial and industrial life, and he knew nothing at first hand about the way in which the country was governed. In spite of this his sweeping generalizations, like those of the early physicists, were efforts of genius. Considering the limitations under which they were produced their predictive value in the short run and in a limited field was high, and it is not surprising that they seemed, like the mechanics of Newton, to require only minor modification and elaboration to meet all predictive requirements. But neither rulers nor ruled behaved as the hypothesis required that they should, and there are good grounds for claiming that, except in terms so vague as to be almost worthless, the Marxist hypothesis is no longer of much value for forecasting economic and political occurrences except in special cases. All the same it is rash to neglect it and in practice no responsible person does so. At the lowest the Communist theory gives an excellent account of what is likely to happen in a capitalist society unless precautions are taken to prevent it.

This raises an interesting point which is frequently overlooked. There is an important difference between predicting the behaviour of human beings and predicting that of physical and non-human biological phenomena. As far as the latter are concerned prediction will not significantly alter their behaviour. It will not affect that of the former either unless they get to know of it, but if they do the situation is altered. Take the prediction of election results. Provided we conceal the conclusions derived from our researches, the situation is much the same as it is in the prediction of any observable event on statistical data. But if we publish them some people may not bother to vote, some may change their vote in order to be on the winning side, and so on. Possibly these decisions will cancel and not affect the accuracy of the prediction, but we cannot be sure about that. We can, however, be sure that if we explain to capitalists, who can hire experts to advise them, that their present course of action will lead to crisis, chaos, and revolution they will take steps to avert these consequences. And this is in fact what has occurred and is occurring. The success of Marx's first approximation led capitalists to look for ways out of his dilemma, and on the whole they have achieved the desired result.

So far the position is this. It is by no means obvious on empirical grounds that workers in the United States and Western Europe need to start revolutions in order to win permanent freedom from poverty and exploitation, and it is still not certain that the reverse is the case. There are good arguments on both sides, but on the whole the weight of the evidence is with the gradualists. It is not, however, convincingly so, and it may justly be regarded as doubtful whether in Asia and Africa it is so at all. What matters is that these are empirical questions which have to be decided on the weight of the evidence. There is no one guaranteed correct answer, and the probabilities in any country do not necessarily remain the same from year to year. Roughly it is the case that left wing non-Marxist Socialists believe that sooner or later revolution will be needed even in Western Europe and the United States, while right wing non-Marxist Socialists think that it will not.

This is where the question of foundations arises. It is perfectly possible to be a right or left wing Socialist without having any foundations. But neither Marx nor his successors, the Russian Bolshevists, would have any truck with this possibility. From their point of view empiricism is a damnable heresy. It is called Opportunism, Kautskyism, Subjectivism, and Social Fascism. At this point we leave Marx the genius and turn to a much less edifying figure, Marx the Communist theologian.

The distinction, indeed, is not clear-cut. Marx, Engels, and Lenin themselves frequently inveigh against doctrinaire adherence to abstract principles as contrasted with empirical study of the facts or, as they prefer to call it, objective assessment of the concrete situation. Lenin in particular praised the revolutionary zeal but deplored the utopianism of those Left-wing Communists who in the 1920s advocated refusal to co-operate with bourgeois political parties on the ground that this would compromise their Communist faith. He wrote as follows (*Left Wing Communism*, 1920): 'After the first Socialist revolution of the proletariat, the proletariat of that country *for a long time* remains *weaker* than the bourgeoisie . . . It is possible to conquer the more powerful enemy only by exerting the utmost effort . . . by taking advantage of every antagonism of interest among the bourgeoisie of the various countries; by taking advantage of every opportunity of gaining a mass ally, even though this ally be temporary, vacillating, unstable, unreliable, and conditional. Those who do not understand this fail to understand even a grain of Marxism and of scientific, modern Socialism in general . . . This applies equally to the period before and the period after the conquest of political power by the proletariat. Our theory is not a dogma but a guide to action.'

Machiavelli himself could not improve on this, and it is by no means an isolated passage. But alongside it and combined with much excellent practical advice on how to run a successful conspiracy for achieving power by legal and illegal methods, which deserves most careful study by the police in non-Communist countries, there is always the conviction that there are foundations of Marxism which must be maintained at all costs against heretics and unbelievers. The sole aim is to achieve power and to retain it, but those who are squeamish about the methods recommended for the purpose may reassure themselves by reference to the foundations. There they will discover that the establishment and maintenance of the dictatorship of the proletariat is not merely inevitable but eminently praiseworthy.

The foundation of Communism is a modified version of the Hegelian dialectic. Marx himself maintained that Hegel's version was upside down and that what he had done was to turn it the right way up. What he had in mind was that Hegel had conceived dialectical development as something essentially mental or spiritual and had thus been led to ignore or minimize the importance of economic factors in political developments. Marx wanted to reverse this and, largely under the influence of Feuerbach's materialism, to make mental operations of all sorts causally dependent on physical changes. Probably what he really wanted was something very like the Physicalist theory developed by the Vienna Circle in the nineteen-thirties, but he was in no position to achieve this type of view because the scientific methodology of his time was largely mistaken and because his own knowledge of what was going on in contemporary science was rudimentary.

It is admitted even by Hegel's ardent admirers that the weakest part of his system is his *Philosophy of Nature*, and this is bound to be the case. As long as one talks vaguely about psychological processes and developments one can use 'contradiction' and 'negation' as the names of queer causes without obviously talking nonsense, and one can be undecided as to whether these causes are (1) metaphysical in the sense of being somehow more fundamental than ordinary causes but not in any way replacing them or interfering with them; (2) on the same level as ordinary causes but supplementary to them in the confused sense in which Divine interference with natural laws by miracles has sometimes been supposed to occur; (3) genuine causes, that is, what scientists ought to look for in nature. (1) is harmless but vacuous since no difference whatever is made to scientific or other investigations by the acceptance of it. (2) is relatively innocuous. Philosophers can look for dialectical causes if they want to. They merely waste their time and do no harm. (3) is noxious since it is a demand that philosophers and not scientists should formulate the aim and method of scientific inquiry. Marx unfortunately was not satisfied with (1) or even with (2); he wanted (3). His foundations, though they are logically worthless, are not metaphysical and harmless in the sense in which those of the democrats and Hegelians are. They are, and are intended to be, extremely practical. The contrast I am trying to make here is one which concerns psychology rather than logic, since I maintain that the Dialectic, whether manipulated by Hegel or by Marx, is incapable of providing good reasons for any political action or inaction. But it is essential to remember that Marx did not hold this view. A great part of his criticism of the Hegelians is to be found in his doctrine that philosophers hitherto had only interpreted the world whereas what was needed was to change it.

In this contention Marx was certainly correct, though whether it was reasonable to criticize philosophers in general and Hegelians in particular for failing to give political prescriptions is another question. Hegel at any rate had certainly said: 'One word more about giving instruction as to what the world ought to be. Philosophy in any case always comes on the scene too late to give it. As the thought of the world it appears only when actuality is already there cut and dried after its process of formation has already been completed – the owl of Minerva spreads its wings only with the falling of the dusk.' Indeed he regarded the Dialectic as a description of the development of Mind or Spirit and held that human intelligence could do no more than recognize and give an account of this development *ex post facto*. Hence, though his dialectical theorizing did not exclude revolutions, it was by no means a warrant for making them. Its tendency was to discourage and not to promote upheavals.

Marx might have attacked Hegelianism and the political recommendations which claimed to be based on it by the kind of empirical arguments I have set out above. He did not do so. He chose to set a metaphysic to catch a metaphysic and to attack Hegel with his own favourite weapon. He transformed the Dialectic from a theory of the development of Spirit to a theory of the development of the means of production and attempted to demonstrate as a necessary and not an empirical truth that feudalism *had* to be succeeded by capitalism and that capitalism *had* to yield to communism.

What he never saw, owing mostly to his muddled use of 'negation', is that this just cannot be done. We can if we choose to do so use 'negation' to stand indifferently for (a) logical denial; (b) physical opposition; (c) any kind of difficulty or incompatibility that can occur. But this is merely a mystifying linguistic trick. We have not given any new factual information when we say that the oak tree negates the acorn, steam negates water, or capitalism negates feudalism. And it is not helpful to talk about the inner contradictions of feudalism and capitalism when what we mean is simply that these forms of economic and political organization tend to lead to difficulties which those who adopt them may not be clever or determined enough to overcome.

None the less the dialectic like other intellectual devices can be made to look as if it worked by a careful choice of definitions and of suitable rules for manipulating them. It is not strictly speaking a method of solving puzzles, since we have to know the answer before we can see how to achieve it by means of the method. But when we do know the answer, we always can invent a dialectical process for reaching it. Thus we can 'prove' that there must really be two classes and only two in society, namely exploiters and exploited, bourgeoisie and proletarians. If there seem to be more, that is just an illusion or a vestigial relic of a stage of development which has practically disappeared. We can 'prove' that there must be a period of capitalism between feudalism and Communism. And if as in the Russian revolution this seems not to have been the case, we say again that appearances are deceptive. There was such a period but it was a very short one, and so on. Furthermore we can have bitter controversies as to what is the correct dialectical account to give of historical events for which the explanations in the ordinary historical sense are perfectly well known.

What it all leads to is a historicism much more vicious and misleading than that of Hegel himself or of any of the other practitioners who have specialized in historical determinism. For the genuine Marxist is committed to saying that capitalists and proletarians are somehow forced or compelled to behave in certain predictable ways. Capitalist democracy must lead to unemployment and war, and the United States must attack and attempt to destroy the U.S.S.R. There is nothing merely probable about this. It is not predicted empirically by studying economic trends and tendencies. It has to happen because the dialectic requires that it should happen. All that the trends and tendencies can reveal is that it will probably happen in 1953 rather than in 1955 or 1960. It is the most startling instance of the way in which the working of an abstract postulational system and a fallacious one at that can lead intelligent people to act in such a way as to try to make its predictions work.

It is unnecessary to pursue this matter further here. Suitable definitions of 'labour', 'profit', and other words make it easy to 'prove' that all profits are the result of immoral (but inevitable) exploitation, that the bourgeoisie must go on oppressing the proletariat, that revolution is inevitable and that the good proletarians are certain to defeat the wicked employers in the end. There are however two pieces of dialectical demonstration which deserve a little more attention. The first is the argument against any sort of gradualism or empirical approach to political difficulties, the second is the doctrine that it is impossible and not just unwise or inexpedient to adapt or modify the capitalist State to suit communist requirements. Both these suggestions are dreadful heresies which Marx and Lenin after him involved themselves in violent and interminable controversies to eradicate, and both are technically interesting as illustrations of the place which discussions about foundations play in Marxist intellectual activities and of the interaction of metaphysical with empirical reasonings in the formation of communist policy.

Gradualism is excluded because dialectical development proceeds by discrete jumps. You cannot have half a negation. And since by definition communism negates capitalism, there can be no compromise between them. More precisely the ideas of capitalism and communism are fundamentally opposed. It is therefore impossible for Capitalists even if they want to do so to satisfy the inevitable claims of the workers. Hence it follows that social security legislation and welfare States must be swindles. They must be just camouflage behind which the progressive exploitation of workers by capitalists goes on unabated, and the more they look as if they were the real thing the more detestable they are. It takes a good deal of natural piety to make this sound plausible, but the foundations are such that the effort has to be made. Incidentally one may note here that Marx has substantially changed Hegel's account of the way in which the dialectical process works. Hegel's syntheses do not just obliterate the theses and antitheses which they supersede. They transcend, incorporate, or 'sublate' them. Thus in Collingwood's language, the past is preserved or 'incapsulated' in the present. In so far as this is believed, it does at least make sense, though it is rather misleading to talk of one historical situation or type of organization following inevitably on another (though historical and logical inevitability are not the same sort of thing). But this is not what Marx means. Capitalism is not incorporated in communism. It is annihilated by it. The transaction is explosive and catastrophic. But then the necessity by which the two are said to be connected ceases to be anything more than a purely verbal one. In fact the dialectic has to be remodelled in order to yield the refutation of gradualism, and the remodelling robs it of the plausibility which vagueness previously lent it. It is now on the face of it just a trick with definitions which has no force except in purely verbal disputations.

The argument concerning the State is on much the same lines. It is important to Marx to dispose of democratic and Hegelian theories, according to which the laws of existing States ought generally to be obeyed though many of them admittedly require amendment and improvement. Hence a firm redefinition of 'State' is called for. What has to be done is to distinguish sharply between 'State' and 'Society'. The latter now becomes applicable to the types of human associations in which political philosophers ought to be interested. 'England', 'France', 'the United States', and so on, are the names of Societies. 'State' is reserved for something more like the government by which a particular Society is ruled. Now by definition Society consists of two classes, exploiters and exploited, and between these there can be no compromise. Hence it is mere bourgeois misrepresentation to suggest that the government (including police, soldiers, civil servants, and officials generally) can represent or look after the interests of Society as a whole. There are and can be no such interests. There are the completely opposed interests of the two classes and the government represents the interests of the oppressors only. Hence it follows that the State is simply a committee for managing the affairs of the bourgeois class. Now what the revolution does is to replace the bourgeois ruling class by the proletariat. The bourgeois State is annihilated and in its place a proletarian government comes into being. It is therefore misguided to say that the capitalist system might be taken over or adapted. Only gradualists and vulgarizers talk like that. An entirely new system is created.

But here there is what looks like a technical hitch. For one had been led to suppose that what the dialectic demanded was the triad feudalism, capitalism, communism (that is, classless society). What we now learn is that capitalism is replaced by a dictatorship of the proletariat. It is only later that, in Engels' much quoted phrase, the State withers away and the classless society is realized. So we get a different triad, namely capitalist dictatorship, proletarian dictatorship, classless society, and the second move here is not a revolution like the first but is described simply as a withering away, which sounds rather gradualist and un-dialectical. Now the empirical reasons for this are clear enough. The apocalyptic vision of the *Communist Manifesto* is too simple to fit the facts. In order to abolish a régime it is necessary in practice not merely to make a revolution but to defend it. It can be only in the very long run that the government of men is to be replaced by the administration of things, and this can happen only if all traces of the previous régime are conscientiously obliterated.

But the dialectical foundations cannot easily be adapted to support this practical conclusion and savage controversies are involved in the process. Marx's writings on the Paris Commune of 1870 and the greater part of Lenin's *State and Revolution* are admirable instances of this. But the writings of all the great communists from Marx to Stalin are full of them. Anyone who is acquainted with these diatribes and who is neither a Marxist nor a theologian will agree that they are reminiscent of the least edifying wrangles over abstract points of doctrine in the history of the Church. Thus Lenin devotes pages of savage vituperation to refuting the view (maintained by Kautsky) that Engels's remark about 'withering away' was a concession to gradualism. The whole theory of proletarian dictatorship is expounded and the dialectical foundations are carefully restated.

One feels that this kind of thing is all very well, but what on earth has it got to do with the barricades? The Russian revolution was a staggering success, so why worry about whether it involved going straight from feudalism to the dictatorship of the proletariat without stopping at bourgeois capitalism on the way? If a revolution succeeds after abolishing the existing machinery of government, or after taking over some of it, or if it fails in spite of doing all the right things because the forces of counter-revolution are too powerful or too strongly supported from abroad, what does it matter whether the events which take place can be explained by means of the sacred writings and the dialectical foundations? In short, why not stop wrangling about useless foundations and get on with the job? How much one sympathizes with Lenin's postscript (written in December, 1917), 'It is more pleasant and useful to go through the experience of the revolution than to write about it' and how different is the tone of *Left Wing Communism, an Infantile Disorder* from that of *Empirio-Criticism!*

Perhaps this reveals one of the reasons why communist disputes about foundations have been so numerous and so bitter. They are like the quarrellings of generals between wars about strategic principles. When nothing much is happening it is a fact of psychology that party leaders tend to quarrel with one another and parties and governments tend to disintegrate. And the interval between 1870 and 1917 interrupted only by the unsuccessful Russian attempt of 1905 was a very long one in which the Fabians on the whole were doing quite well and the Communists seemed to be getting nowhere.

A further psychological point is that Marx and Engels were Germans arguing with Germans, and most of Lenin's opponents were German or German-educated. And it just is a fact that many Germans tend to be devoted to verbal disputes. They and their fellow travellers in other countries are always reluctant to discuss proposals for improving anything without starting from 'the Idea of a State' or 'the Idea of a University' or 'the Idea of a football club.' Hence the verbal wrangles about dialectic seemed less pointless to them than they do to us. It must also be remembered that other political programmes as we have seen had foundations. Hence it was not unreasonable to try to demolish these and substitute others which would support a programme of revolution. And since foundations were so well thought of in the nineteenth century, it seemed important that those of communism should if possible be solid but that at least that they should be agreed.

But these points, though they are important, are not fundamental. The true root of the trouble is a misconception of scientific method. Marx was no more wrong than anybody else on this but most of his successors are disastrously unwilling to admit his error. Engels indeed in *Anti-Dühring* (1878) is sound enough in his criticisms of all claims to formulate incorrigible and final truths other than truisms either in the natural or the sociological sciences. Many of his criticisms of the rigid and closed concepts employed by contemporary physics and biology, with which he was quite well acquainted though, as he admits himself, he was not at all an expert in any of them, are perfectly sound. The difficulty here as elsewhere in Marxism is that 'dialectical' is itself weakened and watered down till it means little more than 'un-mechanical' or 'anti-dogmatic'. Had this line been pursued, gradualism would have been the inevitable outcome. It was not pursued. Marx himself would certainly have rejected it if he had lived long enough to consider its implications, for if the criterion of usage is the requirements of actual scientists, it soon becomes evident that both 'materialism' and 'dialectical', in any positive and definite sense, are useless words. Together with their alleged antitheses, 'idealism' and 'mechanism', they can be discarded without loss. This, however, would not do at all. Marx wanted demonstrations based on indubitable premises and was in principle friendly to the dogmatic claims of Victorian science. He thought they could be squared with the equally dogmatic claims of his Dialectic to refute Idealism and Mechanism (which Engels called Empiricism). Subsequent developments have reinforced this attitude. Lenin, partly because Ernst Mach, who was a positivist and had much influence over the early Vienna Circle, was also a gradualist, was extremely dogmatic over science; and his descendants have not hesitated, except possibly in the sphere of nuclear physics, to prescribe the party line to scientific investigators. Yet it is inherent in the Marxist view itself that any statement about politics should be a provisional hypothesis and not a revealed Last Word. For communists as much as anybody else are historically conditioned. Their ideology is simply the reflexion of the economic conditions of production prevailing when they write. They can no more transcend their historical environment and write like angels than feudal or capitalist writers can. Of course this is admitted up to a point. Lenin and Stalin have gained much glory by showing how the Marxist foundations can be adapted to deal with situations which in the nature of things Marx and Engels could not foresee. Hence the somewhat cumbersome title 'Marxism-Leninism-Stalinism' by which the foundations are now officially known to the faithful.

But the foundations themselves, that is the general metaphysic of dialectical materialism, are regarded as sacred, unalterable, and timeless truths about the nature of the world. In precisely the same way the axioms of Euclid and the Newtonian laws of motion were regarded as sacred, unalterable, and timeless truths about matter of fact until scientists and logicians demonstrated that they were nothing of the kind. But communists have not so far moved with the times. Hence we have the bizarre spectacle of the political theory which above all else claims to be tough and scientific fiercely repudiating as 'bourgeois science' the positivist attitude towards axioms and presuppositions which scientists outside the U.S.S.R. unanimously accept. It is the Marxist devotion to science which makes the early battles over foundations intelligible and the present-day worship of them ludicrous.

Marxist foundations then are worthless. Either they are metaphysical and empty, for 'Everything is matter' and 'Everything is mind' are alike meaningless since there is no way of proving them true or false, or they are short cuts, half-truths, and first approximations of a semi-scientific kind which in themselves have little or no predictive value except for a short time and in special circumstances. Capitalists are notoriously cunning and intelligent in selecting the agents they employ, and it is therefore significant that bankers, traders, and manufacturers all over the civilized world keep economists and statisticians, not expert dialectical materialists, as their advisers.

§5. *Philosopher kings*

The ideologies or foundations which have been discussed in the last three sections all pretend to give intellectual support to different types of political organization and legislative policy. Essentially they are systems of axioms and definitions selected for this purpose. The trouble is that they are either so vague that no practical conclusions can be drawn from them (though they will cover almost any programme which is recommended on empirical grounds) or so precise as to be by no means obviously sound and to be indistinguishable from ordinary laws or scientific hypotheses. The idea of the philosopher king is of a different type. It is usually evoked in connexion with monarchy but it really involves a view as to ruling in general. There are two main forms of it, one intellectual and one anti-intellectual. The first is best stated by Plato, the second is the basis of many dictatorships and was the basis of the *Führerprinzip* of the German Third Reich.

The Platonic view is well-known and persuasive. Although it is a mistake generated by common verbal usage, it deserves serious consideration because the error involved is widespread. The argument is as follows. Doctors, farmers, generals, engineers, and other professional men all possess special kinds of technical knowledge. Indeed it is the possession of this knowledge which entitles them to be called by these names. Hence it is reasonable to suppose that ruling, which is also a professional job, has some specialized knowledge associated with it. There must be some body of truths with which rulers are acquainted and of which other people are ignorant, and it is because they have this special type of knowledge that rulers are called 'rulers'. It is then an important part of the function of political philosophy to ascertain just what this knowledge is and to impart it to those who are or are going to become rulers. But at this point there is a difficulty. It is not at all easy to say what this special knowledge is or how it might be acquired.

At first sight there is an easy way out. Obviously rulers need the sort of knowledge which Aristotle and Machiavelli imparted. They need to know the kinds of conduct which tend to produce success and disaster. 'If you decide to hurt somebody you must do the job so thoroughly that neither he nor his associates will ever be in a position to revenge themselves on you.' 'Be careful never to antagonize the middle classes.' 'Take care to bribe the right members of the opposition.' There are plenty of tips of this kind which it is most valuable for rulers to know. But that is not what Plato had in mind. It is the kind of specialized knowledge that election agents and party managers are supposed to have. Monarchs, Prime Ministers, and statesmen generally are ill-advised to ignore it, but only in the same way as they are ill-advised to ignore the advice of their economists, statisticians, and General Staff. The possession of it is what is said to characterize an astute politician rather than a statesman. Much the same may be said about high grade administrative ability, strategic genius, and other gifts. Rulers do not need to possess these though they may do so. But they need experts who do possess them and whose advice they can obtain. Government by experts is not usually good government just because experts tend to be obsessed by their own expertise and to ignore points of view which differ from their own. Yet it clearly will not do to say that the special knowledge which the ruler wants is a superficial acquaintance with a lot of subjects, just enough to enable him to understand what his experts are talking about.

Hence Plato concluded that what the statesman needed was not knowledge of any special branch or branches of study. It was knowledge of a reality of a higher order. What the ruler must have was knowledge of the Idea of the Good, and this was the subject on which the philosopher was required to instruct him. But again there is a difficulty because neither Plato nor anyone else has ever been able to say except in metaphorical and mystical language how the phrase 'the Idea of the Good' is used. Either it has the same emptiness as other metaphysical phrases like 'the Absolute' and 'the Dialectic' or it is given some content, and then we find that what the ruler is being told to do is simply to attend to some special branch of study such as moral philosophy or public administration. What else, after all, is there left for him to do?

This formulation of the case is partly right and partly wrong. It is right in that 'doctor', 'engineer', and 'ruler', though they look the same kind of words, are of different logical types. They do not differ in the crude way in which 'a right-hand glove and a left-hand glove' differs from 'a pair of gloves'. It is perfectly significant to say 'Sir Winston Churchill is both a great statesman and a strategic genius'. But error arises when it is assumed that 'being a statesman' and 'being a general' stand for strictly comparable activities. 'Ruling' describes an activity, but a different type of activity from cooking and engineering.

What goes wrong with the Platonic view is that, having rightly noted this discrepancy, it assumes that there must be some object or objects with which rulers are familiar, and as this object is not among the recognized objects of human study it must be somewhere else, namely in the shadow world of Universals. Admittedly this is not very helpful since we cannot say anything about this Idea of the Good with which the statesman is familiar. Whenever we try to do so we find that we have missed it and are talking about everyday studies again. But perhaps that is only because we have not tried hard enough, and what we should do is to gird the philosophical loins and make another attempt.

Fortunately however these rather despairing efforts are not necessary. It is not particularly hard to describe what rulers do. They exercise authority and make decisions. Rulers of States do not differ from rulers of other kinds of association except in that the decisions they have to make are more important and therefore the responsibility for making them is particularly heavy. Nobody supposes that the captain of a cricket or football team has some special bits of knowledge about the game which other players on the side do not have. Very often the opposite is the case. There is no harm in saying 'He knows how to exercise authority' provided it is clearly understood that this does not convey the same type of factual information as 'He knows how to give a reverse pass' or 'to bowl leg breaks'. An important part of the difference is that anyone who is not mentally or physically deficient can be taught how to play golf, drive a motor car, or do long division up to a modest standard of proficiency, but there are plenty of eminent athletes and scholars who can never learn how to keep the Lower Shell in order for half an hour.

Plato's mistake here as so often was the typically Greek mistake of over-intellectualization. He never wavered in his belief that deductive theorizing was the only human activity which was perfectly respectable and appropriate to a gentleman. And since statesmanship was obviously respectable it must in the end be found to consist in some kind of theorizing. So ruling had to be the exercise of a kind of theoretical activity, and therefore there had to be a special sphere named 'the Idea of the Good' about which this type of theoretical activity was concerned. It would be most unfair to blame Plato much for this mistake. It is still commonly made by examination boards, interviewing committees, and believers in I.Q. tests as reliable evidence of powers of leadership.

The other type of error about ruling is much more dangerous though again it contains something of the truth. What Hitler and his kind correctly recognize is that the ability to do theoretical calculations does not in itself constitute capacity to govern. Then wrongly assuming that this ability is something for which rulers have no use either in themselves or in their advisers they fall back on intuitive certainties and try to think with their blood. This is seldom successful for long. To say that calculation is not enough is not the same as to say that it is waste of time. Intuitive ruling may do very well for the village cricket side and the primitive tribe, but it leads to trouble when it is trusted in complicated associations like modern States.

Most of the current mistakes about ruling, then, are due to an imperfect grasp of the factual situation, a confusion between it and other activities which bear a superficial resemblance to it; and this confusion is encouraged and made persistent by the linguistic usage which suggests that there is a special body of theoretical knowledge which rulers in general and rulers of States in particular should possess and in which philosophers are peculiarly qualified to give instruction. But a little empirical investigation will show that the only instruction in ruling which philosophers have ever given has been instruction in elementary psychology, political institutions, and party management. They have also talked about moral philosophy and the foundations of politics, but rulers seem on the whole to have paid little attention to this part of the syllabus.

Nevertheless the philosopher king is a helpful supplement to the notion of political foundations. As we have seen these are necessarily vague and abstract. They have to be translated into actual legislation, and it looks as if some special skill is needed to do this. Hence the notion of the semi-divine or inspired legislator is always useful. Lycurgus, Stalin, and the Supreme Court of the United States have all been cast for this part though the foundations they have accepted look widely different. Sometimes on the other hand it appears that identical foundations are appealed to in support of diametrically opposed policies. To take an instance at random, President Truman, addressing the Foreign Ministers of the American Republics on March 26th 1951, asserted that 'the two principles which had long been the basis of relations between the American Republics were a belief that "international affairs should be based upon co-operation among free and independent nations, and not upon coercion or force", and a conviction that "the aim and purpose of government is to promote the welfare of all the people – not just the privileged few".' There is nothing here to which any representative of the Soviet Union would take exception, yet Truman and Stalin were not agreed as to policy. This confirms the view that philosopher kings are either ordinary political counsellors with no special qualifications for the job or vendors of solemn phrases which can be employed to make any policy look more or less respectable.

CHAPTER 5

Empirical Politics

§1. *The menace of scepticism*

THE criticism I have directed against traditional political philosophy and against the supposed foundations of democratic political institutions will seem shocking to many readers. Even those who feel that there may well be something in it may consider that it is ill-timed and in poor taste. It is indeed precisely the line of thought which has been in recent years heavily attacked as tending to undermine our faith in Western culture and civilization, and the commonest line of criticism developed against it from this point of view may be stated as follows. The culture which has grown up in Western Europe and the United States during the last three thousand years or so is valuable. It is important to preserve it. Philosophers should contribute to this end by discovering the political principles on which this culture rests and demonstrating that they are theoretically sound. It is therefore a kind of intellectual treason to suggest that there are no such principles and that what have been supposed to be the foundations of our political institutions are really not foundations at all. To criticize them except in a harmless academic way which produces no objections except those to which satisfactory answers can be given is somehow to sell the pass. Put bluntly what this comes to is 'If you haven't got a way of life to recommend to your readers and some philosophical arguments with which to support it, you had much better keep quiet. The Communists have both, and as the young in particular demand that kind of thing they are very likely to succumb to the Communist appeal unless you have something convincing to offer in its place.' It is fair to add that precisely the same type of objection is made by representative Marxist authors. To them, however, criticism of foundations appears as a last attempt by the decadent bourgeoisie to undermine the scientific principles on which the work of Marx and Engels is so firmly based.

This type of criticism deserves consideration. It can be made much more plausible than I have made it in a deliberately crude presentation. 'Scepticism' and 'destructive criticism' sound rather frightening, and perhaps after all one ought not to be too rude to accepted views, even if they are wrong, unless one has an alternative of some kind to recommend. It is surely dangerous even if it is true to maintain that the intellectual heritage of Greece which has so long been accepted as the great foundation of Western culture is now a liability and not an asset.

I believe that the alarm and despondency to which empiricism in political thinking gives rise in so many quarters is the outcome of confusion and not of any genuine threat. But before I go into this there is one general remark about it which is worth making, and that is that it is not very original. It is just the kind of criticism that in the great days of Greece Plato levelled at the Sophists and Aristophanes at Socrates. More recently it is what the traditionalists (or rationalists as they are sometimes called) said about Hume and about Kant at the end of the eighteenth century.

In a general way it is easy enough to dispose of it, and Kant himself has given the answer quite clearly. The arguments (or foundations) with which he was primarily concerned in this connexion were the traditional demonstrations of the existence of God, the freedom of the will, and the immortality of the soul. He demolished these and was duly accused of promoting religious scepticism and generally undermining faith and destroying established values. His answer is this: 'Notwithstanding the loss of its fancied possessions which speculative reason must suffer, general human interests remain in the same position as before, and the advantages which the world has derived from the teaching of reason is in no way diminished. The loss affects only the monopoly of the Schools, not the interests of humanity. I appeal to the most rigid dogmatist, whether the proof of the continued existence of the soul after death, derived from the simplicity of substance, or of the freedom of the will as opposed to universal mechanism, arrived at by the subtle but ineffectual distinction between subjective and objective practical necessity, or of the existence of God as deduced from the concept of an *ens realissimum* (of the contingency of the changeable and the necessity of a prime mover) have ever upon passing out from the Schools succeeded in reaching the public mind or in exercising the slightest influence upon its convictions. That has never been found to occur and ought never to have been expected.' In other words, if people are becoming sceptical about religion it is not because they have discovered some metaphysical foundations are worthless. They never knew or cared about these.

The analogy between this controversy and the contemporary debate on political foundations is clear enough. It is true that Victorian clergymen as described in *The Way of All Flesh* sometimes claimed to have lost their faith because they had come to doubt the validity of their Orders; and that is rather like what would happen if the citizens of Massachusetts claimed to have lost faith in their democratic institutions because they had found out that the Mayflower Compact of Society was after all an ingenious invention. But somehow the 'because' in both these statements seems to be wrong. When people say that sort of thing one suspects that they are just making an excuse. What has really happened is that they have ceased to believe in the institution on other and better grounds. It has lost its authority.

The case of politics, however, is not quite parallel to these since as we have seen political slogans like 'natural rights', 'exploitation', and the rest do get beyond the Schools and make a difference to observable conduct. But this is not important here since in such cases it is the slogans themselves

with their emotional appeal and not the theoretical arguments
which are alleged to justify them that matter.

All this, however, is preaching and not argument. What
in detail is the case for maintaining that attempts to discover the foundations of politics are valuable and should
not be discarded, as I am trying to do? For it may be said,
'Even if these proofs do not work, it is the job of the philosopher not just to show that they don't but to look for others
that do. It is wrong simply to throw in the hand.' The real
motive here is mostly fear of a bogey called 'subjectivism'
and this has to be disposed of before further progress can
be made.

§2. *Subjectivism*

Precisely what is meant by describing a view about politics
or morals as 'subjectivist' or as 'involving subjectivism' is
usually far from clear, but what is vaguely asserted by those
who use this language is something like this. Unless we can
produce some valid deductive argument in favour of one
variety of political (or moral) institutions, we shall be reduced to saying 'Well, we do things in this way here and
now but people do them differently at other places and
times. It is all a matter of personal preference and you may
please yourself'. After all, we do not usually criticize the
Russians for liking vodka though most of us do not think it
is very nice, so why should we criticize them for liking
concentration camps, direction of labour, one party government, and state ownership of all important property? We
like to have a good deal of personal liberty, they care very
little about it, but that is entirely their affair and it is
impertinent to criticize them for it.

Certainly some people do hold or profess to hold this sort
of view. It had quite a vogue in Germany and elsewhere in
the 1920s, though it lost a lot of appeal when Hitler began
to give practical effect to his personal preferences. When this
happened many of the victims and their relatives quite
properly claimed that he was acting wrongly and were not

satisfied by saying merely that they disagreed with his personal likes and dislikes. Indeed as a view it is obviously hopeless except for those who lead extremely well-protected lives. Yet it is not manifestly a stupid view. The question then is, can it be disposed of without reverting to a doctrine of foundations of some kind? I think that its appeal depends entirely on a serious confusion in the contrast between 'subjective' and 'objective' and that when this is removed there is no cause for alarm.

'Subjective' is generally a disapproving word. It is used in this sort of context as more or less equivalent to 'sceptical', 'personal', and 'private', and it at least suggests superficiality and irresponsibility. When those who make use of it say that an opinion or a judgement is subjective they usually mean 'You cannot prove that or even give any reasons for it. It is just a personal opinion which nobody else need accept if he doesn't like it'.

Objective judgements on the other hand are those which are 'rational'. They have some constraining and compelling force and it is not open to us to accept or reject them at will. They rest on demonstration, not merely on personal idiosyncrasies. We reject them only at the cost of being set down as either fools who cannot follow a valid argument or obstinate knaves who know the answers perfectly well but refuse to admit that they are true.

Just what is the cash value of this distinction?

To explain the matter fully would require a considerable excursion into the history of epistemology, especially in the seventeenth century, which would be out of place here. The root of the trouble is the mistaken search for absolute standards which has already been discussed. With the great advances of science and especially of the application of mathematical technique which dates roughly from Galileo, and with the introduction of the 'new way of ideas' derived from a misunderstanding of the physiology of perception, which became prominent at about the same time, this search took a new turn which has been important and in some ways deleterious for the last three hundred years.

Essentially what the scientists of the sixteenth and seventeenth centuries did was to discover that tremendous advances could be made by weighing and measuring, and generally by skilfully posing and solving mathematical puzzles; and this led to the further reflexion that errors of observation due to the personal peculiarities of observers could largely be avoided or discounted if sufficiently accurate methods of weighing and measuring were introduced. It is only a short step from here to the conclusion that evidence got by looking at things and smelling and touching them is always more or less unreliable. It is personal or subjective, whereas weighing and measuring are impersonal, objective, and truly scientific. Of course there is a difficulty here since weighing and measuring themselves require some sort of observation, even if it is only the recording of pointer readings, but that does not concern us. The point is that by thinking in this way we come easily to accept the results gained by weighing and measuring as the only assessments which are perfectly reliable, and we fail to notice that this assumption is often unjustified.

Thus when I say '$7 \times 9 = 63$', that is objective. There is nothing personal or private about it. When I say 'Jones is 6 feet tall and weighs 17 stone', that is almost wholly objective. It is not quite perfect because actual measuring rods are never beyond criticism, and the person who does the measuring and reads the gauges is subject to personal errors; but it is practically beyond criticism. When I say 'Jones is a good cricketer' I am becoming less objective, but I can still add up the runs he made and the wickets he took last season and they seem at first sight to meet the requirement. When, however, I say 'Jones is good-looking' we are in trouble. It looks as if I must either produce a numerically expressible standard of aesthetic appraisal or admit that I have merely put forward a personal opinion. And the same is alarmingly true of 'Jones is a good man'. That is why writers about politics and morals find the bogey of subjectivism so discouraging.

In fact the demand for 'objective' standards in politics and in morals is simply a demand for a criterion which will enable us to grade people and institutions with the same sort of certainty and confidence as that with which, with very minor qualifications, we can grade physical bodies in terms of size and weight. We would like to appraise actions and constitutions as 'good', 'not so good', and 'bad', with the same simplicity and the same approximation to certainty and infallibility as that which we achieve in grading men as 'more than 6 feet tall' and '6 feet tall or less'. Ideally we aim at the complete certainty and infallibility we have in the case of 'seven is greater than six and six is greater than five'.

At this point, however, we must stop and ask 'Does this demand make any sense?' What does it mean to talk about a criterion of this kind, and are those who cry for it looking for something which they might have but have not got and which would be of value to them if they had it? Or are they looking for something which it is nonsense to ask for at all? The fact that none of the answers put forward is of the slightest use suggests, though it does not prove, that the latter is the case. At any rate it is sobering and instructive in this connexion to reflect on the heroic but unsuccessful efforts of the philosophical radicals and their modern successors to produce simple, workable, and fool-proof criteria of happiness, prosperity, and progress, and of modern moralists to achieve a usable criterion of goodness and obligation.

Yet it should not be forgotten, though theorists seem sometimes to be in danger of forgetting, that quite ordinary people do succeed in using significantly all the appraisal words and statements which I have just introduced. They do not think that when they do so they are just reporting their personal preferences, and they produce reasons in support of their statements. Sometimes they even convince one another without the assistance of the Inquisition and the concentration camp. They manage to do this because they avoid the intellectualist error of pretending that there must be one test and only one test, and that of a simple metrical type which will finally settle or provide objective answers to all proper questions. Of course if we start by saying 'I will accept nothing but a numerical statement or a logical deduction from agreed axioms as a satisfactory answer to my question' we are doomed to get into trouble fairly soon unless the world is much simpler and tidier than we have any reason to suppose that it is. That is just the fallacy of supposing that every difficulty can be replaced by a straightforward puzzle. But ordinary people do not expect to be able to do that. And that is why the subject-ivist bogey is just a bogey. It frightens nobody except its inventors.

To get this clear it is as well to begin with the sort of appraisal question that we do know how to answer and to see how in the normal course of business we set about dealing with it. How then do we settle 'Is X a better full-back or private secretary or operatic soprano than Y?' To begin with, unless the discussion is a pointless one as to whether Bradman was a better bat than W. G. Grace, the question has to be made a good deal more precise before it can be considered at all. Usually we do not notice this because the limitation of scope which is needed is pro-vided by the context. We know whether we are talking about Internationals or about the School 2nd XV. This being granted, the question concerns the procedure of selection committees and there is nothing obscure or diffi-cult about it. Without detailed examination we can, I think, accept two points as needing no further demonstration: (a) there is no single test and no infallible group of tests which will give a final incorrigible answer to this type of enquiry (as there almost is for 'How tall is Jones?'); (b) discussions about such questions are in practice entirely or almost entirely factual. 'I like X better than Y' is not accepted as a valid argument even though one may suspect that the fact which it states has influenced the arguments which a particular selector adduces. But we all know that there are good and bad reasons which can be given in such discussions, and it will not do to say that the position is fundamentally quite simple since the sole aim of selectors is to win a particular game. In real life even games usually present greater difficulties than that.

The process through which appointments boards, selection committees, employers, and other appraising agents normally go in order to achieve their aims is two-fold. In practice both elements often occur simultaneously but for purposes of exposition it is convenient to treat them as successive. First, then, there is what may be called the establishing of dispositions. This is concerned mainly with the characteristics with which writers of testimonials are familiar; 'industrious', 'honest', 'intelligent', 'reliable', 'enterprising', and similar words are those which occur freely in such contexts.

It is at once clear that these words are not of the same type as '6 feet tall' or 'red-headed'. They refer not to single observable characteristics whose presence or absence can be confirmed by a single visual or metrical test. What they tell us about are dispositions or propensities to behave in ways which are only roughly specifiable. The close grammatical resemblance between 'Jones is red-headed' and 'Jones is hard-working' is extremely misleading. What 'Jones is hard-working' tells the selection committee may be translated into something like this. 'As far as my experience goes, Jones tends to arrive at his work early rather than late and leave it late rather than early. He does not often find excuses for going out to get a cup of coffee; he is irritated and not pleased when interrupted; he goes on when he is tired or not feeling particularly fit ... ; and I have no reason to suppose that he will alter in these respects.'

This sort of statement is just as checkable by reference to observed facts as 'He is red-headed', but it does not give the same kind of information; it is not checkable by the same simple technique, and it is on the whole more subject to error and therefore more a matter on which there may be differences of opinion between different observers. Thus it is generally easier to pretend to be hard-working well enough to deceive a casual observer than it is to pretend to be red-headed or to be 6 inches taller than you are. There is however no difference in principle, since there is no limit to the production of fakes and illusory appearances.

Only one distinction seems to arise here and it is relevant not to political philosophy but to epistemology. Statements like 'It is raining now' (made in the open air) and 'The cat is on the mat' (made when the animal is before your eyes) are in a special position since they are not open to doubt or question except in cases of linguistic incompetence or hallucination. They thus differ in a significant way from 'It is raining now' (I can hear it on the roof) and 'The cat is on the mat' (in the next room. I saw it there a moment ago). The point is worth mentioning only because 'objectivity' is sometimes associated with simple observation-statements of the first type. There is no harm in this usage, and if all that is meant by saying that appraisals are subjective is that they are seldom of that type because it frequently makes sense to demand reasons for them, the distinction may be accepted.

Normally however something more serious is intended, and we need to return to the procedure of selection committee to find out what it is. It should now be agreed that what they do is first to establish a number of dispositional propositions or 'if ... then ... ' propositions about the probable behaviour of prospective players or employees under specified conditions. X will probably work hard, kick straight, add up figures correctly, or whatever it may be. Disagreements may occur here and mistakes may be made as we have already seen. Observers are not all equally careful, intelligent, and honest, and candidates do not always run true to form. A man may cease to be hard-working when he gets married and may cease to be honest when he developes a taste for betting. But on the whole there is usually not too much difficulty either in establishing the truth or in reaching agreement as to what it is; and the questions under discussion are wholly factual. They have nothing to do with the wants or emotional state of the selectors.

We now come to the second point, which looks rather more debatable. This is the assessment of the relative importance of the factors considered at the first stage. How much does it matter that X is rather slow or not always very accurate, that Y's health is not completely reliable, and so on? Here there seems to be a difficulty. We do not get or expect the same measure of agreement as we do at the first stage, but we can still have intelligent argument and discussion, and although the conclusions reached are not always equally certain and are therefore more likely to be revised, there is nothing noticeably private, secret, or subjective about them. 'I think this important' is not at all the same as 'I like this'.

What may easily happen however is that people who have not given much thought to this type of question become puzzled and bewildered when they are asked 'Precisely what new fact is asserted by "X is important" which was not asserted by the if... then statements at the earlier level?' For when they cannot answer this they are liable to be told 'The only new fact in question is your personal preference for X over Y, so your judgements "X is important", "X is better than Y" really are subjective after all'. But this is simply a logical swindle. Nobody supposes that when you have finished constructing a cupboard or a motor car you may be left with just two questions to decide: (a) what colour shall we paint it?; (b) shall it be good or bad? Obviously these are not questions of the same type, and getting puzzled about them is rather like getting puzzled as to what the extra thing is that you have bought when you buy not just a right-hand glove and a left-hand glove but a pair of gloves.

The reason why we seem to find a difficulty over appraisal statements that we do not find in metrical statements (X is 6 feet tall) is partly that neither 'X is important' nor 'I like X' gives a specifiable new bit of information about X and partly that there is not and could not conceivably be any general answer to the question 'Precisely what does it mean to say "X is important"?' We can give reasons for saying it in every particular case but we cannot deduce it as a conclusion from a general principle or set of principles. Consideration of what it means to say '- is important', 'It is important that -' and similar phrases, such as 'That is vital, trivial, essential, etc.' will make this clear. Three points deserve attention. (1) Such phrases always refer to a person or a group of people. (2) They assume some context. (3) They are 'more or less', not 'either . . . or', phrases. A typical complete question is 'How important is it to you that you should go to London to-morrow?' and a proper answer is 'It is fairly important. I have an appointment with my dentist and he is going away for his holiday on the day after to-morrow; but it is not vital'. We do not always put all these points in. We do not even know in many cases how to answer questions about them precisely, and our use of 'important' is consequently imprecise. Sometimes it is so vague as to be almost without significance. 'It is important that all children should learn to read and write', 'The preservation of human life is always important' are almost if not completely vacuous. They are attempts to generalize from true and correct statements like 'It is more important that English children to-day should learn to read and write than that they should learn to play the violin'. The generalizations fail because they leave out all reference to context, to degrees, and often even to persons. It therefore makes no sense to look for a universally applicable criterion of importance, and nothing but our addiction to the fallacy of absolute standards leads us to suppose that it does. We do not find this situation at all embarrassing or even surprising in ordinary life. I doubt whether we should find it so in theory if we had not allowed ourselves to accept for speculative purposes the odd doctrine that nothing except mathematical demonstrations can give us genuine reasons. But unconsciously we have come to talk in this kind of way and therefore we tend to accept in theory though not in practice the contemptuous use of 'subjective' to describe our conclusions on all matters which are not settled by a simple, one-track procedure with gauges and measuring rods. But fortunately we do know quite well how to distinguish between selectors who work on genuinely subjective lines (I like X) and those who appraise candidates for selection in a rational way, that is, who can give relevant reasons though not deductive proofs for the correctness of their decisions.

The relevance of this discussion to political philosophy is so far purely negative. My aim is simply to show that the subjectivist bogey is an illusion, and that therefore the dilemma 'Either objective principles or subjectivism and chaos', like most dilemmas, is more alarming than dangerous. Nevertheless the prevalence of the demand for 'objective' tests for the use of examiners and selection committees and the curious methods which are adopted in order to meet it show clearly the panic which the word 'subjectivism' is liable to start and. the deplorable things people may do and advocate in order to escape from it.

This point, though it is extremely important, cannot be further examined here. But if we confine ourselves to political philosophy, it may be argued that even if what I have said about subjectivism is true, it is unnecessary and irrelevant since there is a simple, usable, and objective test by means of which anybody can assess the merits of rival political systems. So it is a waste of time to try to show as I have been doing that we can get along quite well without having such a test. All that we need to do is to decide

whether a particular institution or set of institutions conduces to the promotion of freedom or not. If it does it is a
good thing and is given a high mark. If it does the opposite
it is a bad thing and either gets a low mark or fails altogether.

This sounds very convincing but what it means is far
from clear. We have already seen some of the difficulties
about 'freedom' in Chapter 3, and in what follows I shall be
to some extent repeating what I said then. But confusions
about freedom are so prevalent and so pervasive that this
will do no harm. To begin with it must be remembered that
'Smith is free' and 'Smith is more free than Jones' are not
informative. Until we can answer 'Free from what?', 'Free
to do what?' they tell us nothing at all. Even then in
ordinary usage they are vague. There are plenty of situations in which we are not at all sure whether to use them or
not. 'He didn't have to shoot the man who was black-
mailing him – but I don't see what else he could have
done.' 'He enjoyed setting fire to the haystack so it is
ridiculous to claim that he couldn't help it. He didn't want
to help it. Yet he is a pyromaniac so perhaps he couldn't
really help it after all.' The uncertainty here arises from
genuine lack of knowledge about psychological facts. We
do not know what idiom to use because we are imperfectly
acquainted with the situations we are trying to describe.
'Free' is just like a lot of other words in natural, non-
technical language. There are any number of cases in which
it is clearly correct to use it, namely where no unknown or
extraneous pressure can reasonably be suspected. 'You can
go either by bus or by underground.' And there are plenty
where it is obviously not correct. 'He can't walk. He has
broken his leg.' But there are many others in which the
decision to use it is more or less arbitrary. Usually in cases
where it is correct to say 'He is free to do it' it is also correct
to say 'He can do it if he wants to', and it is also correct
if he does do it to say afterwards 'He did it of his own free
will', 'He was responsible for it'. This usage is rough and

not precise, but it is the usage in which politicians as distinct from psychologists are interested.

In this usage as we have already seen it is true but trivial to say that all laws abridge freedom. They provide extraneous reasons against doing some kinds of action, and if the police are efficient they make it physically impossible to do others. It is also unhelpful to maintain that we might have a situation in which everyone did exactly as he liked, but it would look just as if there were laws because nobody would choose to interfere with anybody else. This sounds sensible only if we confuse rules of associations with regularities in nature. For even if, to state a highly abstract possibility, we were to achieve such a situation, we should have no guarantee whatever that it would continue. And what should we do with the first juvenile delinquent?

The root of the matter is that 'free' is not the specification of a quality and 'freedom' is not an abstract noun standing for the possession of that quality. 'X is wealthy' and 'X has great possessions' are significant and clear enough. So is 'X is more wealthy than Y'. We can assess them for taxation purposes without too much difficulty. We cannot do this with 'free' and 'freedom' because to try to do so is a nonsensical project. 'Freedom' does not unpack as 'wealth' does into the possession of a lot of countable things. It unpacks into a highly complicated account of wants, needs, permissions, and prohibitions. We can add up the prohibitions if it amuses us to do so, but the number of them tells us nothing about freedom in any ordinary use of the word.

This is not to say that political institutions cannot properly be talked about as being 'free' or 'tyrannical'. Of course they can be. But to make sense of this sort of language the word 'important' has to come in again. There are some kinds of command (or prohibition) which it is generally regarded in some countries as important that governments should abstain from giving. It is only when they encroach on this sphere that we normally talk of them

as abridging freedom or threatening liberty, and it seems
to me that common usage is perfectly correct here. One
does no service either to the cause of freedom or that of clear
thinking by using this sort of language about the regulations of the Ministry of Food or the Treasury. It must,
however, be noted that there is no universal and complete
agreement among men or even among the inhabitants of a
particular country at a particular time as to what the limits
of this sphere are. Freedom of thought and freedom of
religion are typical examples. In Western countries most
people consider them very important though few could
state at all precisely what they involve, and there is no
simple test for deciding the extent to which a given set of
institutions provides for or contravenes them.

The relative importance of these spheres of activity as
compared with social and economic security is even less
clear. To say this however is only to say that these are
difficult and complicated questions. They are so complicated
that easy answers to them are unhelpful and no answer is
anything like incorrigible. But there is nothing particularly
'subjective' about the various answers which deserve
consideration and ideological wars have no tendency whatever to prove that one answer is right and another wrong.

What emerges from all this is that the notion of freedom
does not provide the basis for a clear, straightforward
comparison between constitutions or for the intelligent
criticism of legislation. 'Promotion of freedom' and 'restriction of freedom' are significant and useful phrases but
they are also difficult and complicated to analyse. There is
no simple *a priori* method for answering the question 'Which
will this proposed measure tend to do?'

So the promotion of freedom will not do as the one clear
and practical test of the respectability of a given political
system. It is indeed important, and nobody, including
Marxists, disputes this, but it is not enough. You cannot
dispose quickly of communist or social democratic institutions by saying that they tend to abridge freedom because

(a) it is not clear that they do except in the trivial sense we have already considered; (b) even if they do, freedom is not the only important thing in the world. On the other hand it is equally futile to argue that in some trivial or very esoteric sense totalitarianism does not abridge freedom at all. For these reasons the contemporary tendency to use 'The Free World' as the antithesis to 'The Communist World' is not a very happy one. It suggests a dangerously over-simplified contrast. The phrase 'free institutions' which is sometimes employed in an attempt to clarify it is even less defensible.

§3. *Political appraisals*

In this Section I shall develop what has already been said about subjectivism and about the distinction between difficulties and puzzles in order to show the logical character of political appraisals. What needs to be done is to explain the resemblances and differences between 'The political institutions of Switzerland are better than those of Spain' on the one hand and 'Smith is a better full-back than Jones' on the other. This as may be seen by referring to my introduction is a philosophical question. 'Are the political institutions of Switzerland better than those of Spain?' is not. It may be useful to anticipate my conclusion and to say at once that the differences are very slight and the resemblances very great; in other words, I do not believe that by discarding political foundations or ideologies I am logically committed to political scepticism. If this were the case, it might possibly be justifiable to make use of persuasive but invalid arguments in the hope of convincing readers that the ideology of democracy is superior to that of communism. This might be more effective than to say without further pretence 'I like democratic institutions and I want you to like them too'. But matters are not as desperate as this. It is no more paradoxical to say of a man that he is a good judge of political institutions than it is to say that he is a good judge of pictures or of wine. In none of these or of the kindred occupations do judges operate by studying ideal specimens in their heads and comparing these with imperfect copies which they observe. They analyse and appraise the actual specimens presented to them. Such judging is an intelligent performance but it is not a piece of intellectual theorizing. There are methods of doing it which experts use and which they can sometimes elucidate for the benefit of beginners, but there are no infallible rules such that anyone who follows them will certainly get the right answer as there are in long division and elementary algebra. It is not even the case that good judges always agree as to what the answer is, as they do in crossword puzzles and bridge problems. Indeed it is a mistake to use the word 'answer' at all, since this suggests that what is involved is the solution of a puzzle, and it is not the job of art critics or tea tasters to solve puzzles.

There is however an objection to this view which at first sight appears serious and even insuperable. The resemblance between 'Parliamentary Government is a good political institution' and 'Jones is a good full-back' or 'a good doctor' is often said to be only superficial. The chief reason for this contention is that the latter can be confirmed or refuted by reference to an end or purpose whereas the former cannot be confirmed or refuted in this way. Thus it is at least a partial refutation of 'Jones is a good doctor' to demonstrate that a high proportion of his patients have failed to recover. The refutation is not secure because Jones may have been faced with an epidemic or a battle, but still one can say that he is trying to cure people and is rightly judged by his success or failure in achieving that end. In the same way it is part of the job of a full-back to prevent the opposing side from scoring tries; so it is relevant but not conclusive evidence for the truth of 'Jones is a better full-back than Smith' that the latter has had more tries scored against him than the former by sides of approximately equal scoring power. But there is no comparable method of confirming 'Parliamentary Government is a good political institution'. We do not know how to complete 'The aim of political institutions is to ...' in the same way as we can complete 'The aim of doctors is to ...' or 'The aim of full-backs is to ...' As we saw earlier, doctors and full-backs are not as simple as I have here assumed that they are. But even when this is admitted, little seems to be gained since it is claimed that there is no agreement as to what political institutions are for and therefore no usable tests for the assertion that any particular system of them is good or bad.

We may try to get round this difficulty by pointing out that political institutions are sets of rules and that 'Parliamentary Government is a good political institution' should be compared with statements about the offside rule or the six-ball over or the National Health Service rather than with appraisals of particular practitioners. But this does not get us out of trouble. For the origin of these rules is traceable to the fact that some people want to play games and most people want to be cured of their diseases. Hence the goodness or badness of the rules can be assessed in the light of their provable tendency to produce a given result.

This argument however is not convincing. I can seldom answer 'What is the aim of that rule?' with the same confidence as I can answer 'What is that man trying to do?' or even 'What does that kind of man try to do?' Indeed I am usually far from confident about the answer to 'What result were those who framed this rule trying to prevent or to achieve?' Nevertheless, I am prepared to admit that I usually know the sort of answer which would be adequate in such cases. The aim of the National Health Service is not in doubt. The desirability of it as a political institution is open to challenge and cannot be so easily elucidated.

Two questions then need to be considered. (1) Have political institutions (or the people who devise them) aims or ends or purposes? (2) If they have not, does this compel us to say that political appraisals are completely different from other kinds of appraisal and to admit that the former are subjective or a matter of purely personal preference in a sense in which the latter are not?

Several kinds of answer can be given to 'Why are you (is he) doing that?' or 'Why do you (does he) do that?'

(a) There is no reason for it. It is a habit or trick or mannerism. (Tying the left shoe-lace before the right one.)

(b) I enjoy doing it. (Eating strawberries; playing football.)

(c) In order to get something else. (Going to London to see the dentist; playing football to make money.)

(d) I have an obligation. (I promised Jones that I would meet him.)

Any of these except (a) may be given as the reason for imposing a new rule. Some people enjoy inventing rules (Kant is an instance), others promise their constituents that they will vote for prohibition if they are elected. But generally speaking the answer given to 'Why did you make that rule?' is of type (c) (which does not exclude (b) or (d)); 'Because it will promote the general good (or the good of football players) and it is my aim to promote that good'.

Now 'Aspirins relieve headache' and 'Parliamentary Institutions promote the general good' look very much alike. Hence it is easy to assume that relieving headaches and promoting the general good are both aims or ends and that taking aspirins and adopting Parliamentary institutions are means which we adopt to achieve those ends. But this is an error, as we can see by putting the further question 'How do you know?' or 'What evidence have you for that statement?' Every proper statement of the form X is a means to Y can be supported by empirical evidence showing that X produces or tends to produce Y, and this evidence is statistical. It is of the form n per cent of the people who have headaches and who take aspirins find that their headaches are relieved.

Similarly if the National Health Service is considered as a

health-promoting institution, its success or failure is demonstrable by reference to infant mortality rates, decreases in the incidence of infectious diseases and so on. But it still makes sense to admit that from this point of view it is successful but to condemn it as a political institution. Yet if I say 'I know that the National Health Service reduces infant mortality but I deny that it conduces to the general good', my statement is quite intelligible but demands for statistical evidence in support of it seem to be inappropriate. In the same sort of way I may show that compulsory collective farms and compulsory education tend to raise the general standard of living of a given community and this may be accepted as a truth about economic organization. But my hearers may significantly say that neither conduces to an increase in the general good.

The reason for this embarrassing situation is that we are mistaken in supposing that 'the general good' stands for an end which can be achieved, like healing sickness or scoring goals. What it does stand for is best elucidated by considering how we talk about a type of activity different from that of making and appraising political institutions in which also the analysis into means and ends breaks down, namely the activity of the artist and that of the art critic.

The resemblance here is clear enough. A man may paint a picture or write a book or compose a string quartet because he likes doing that sort of thing or because he wants to make some money or because he has promised to do it. But most people would agree that he may have another reason which is different from these (though not inconsistent with any of them) and much more difficult to describe satisfactorily. Indeed it is fair to infer from the numberless unsuccessful attempts which have been made to elucidate it that no short or simple answer will be adequate. The language of 'calling' and 'vocation' has something to be said for it since it avoids the notion of means and ends as well as that of a casual choice between alternatives. It is unsatisfactory because it suggests something supernatural and mysterious. To say that the artist has to paint or compose also conveys something of the truth but is misleading in that it suggests some sort of external compulsion. We can avoid this by talking in terms of 'expression', but this is too vague to be helpful. It is unnecessary to pursue this discussion further. My aim is simply to show that the language in which we talk about aesthetics indicates our recognition of an activity which is not unimportant and which is neither obligatory nor a means to some end beyond itself.

The same sort of thing can be said about statesmanship, though there are relevant differences which must be noted. Let us however take the resemblances first. It is not an accident that statesmen from Solon to Stalin have commonly commanded respect and even veneration. To say of anyone that he is a statesman or even that his behaviour is statesmanlike is to say that he does or tries to do something important. It means something quite different from what is meant by calling him a politician. We should normally withdraw 'statesman' and substitute 'politician' if we were convinced that Stalin's career was wholly explicable in terms of casual preference ('He plays at politics' or 'He likes that kind of life') or that he was actuated solely by a desire to make money or found a dynasty; nor do we suppose that he promised anybody to behave as he has done. In fact it seems appropriate to talk about him in the same sort of language as we use in discussing Rembrandt or Beethoven. This implies no liking for or even approval of his work. One may loathe Van Gogh but still regard him as a great artist, and Milton's Satan is not a petty or contemptible character.

In all these cases 'What is he doing that for?' is a meaningless question. Grammatically it can be answered by 'In order to promote the general good of the Athenians or the Russians' or 'In order to add to the number of beautiful pictures in the world'. One may also say 'He wants to realize Goodness or Beauty'. But these and similar answers give us no new information. Statesmen and artists, to judge from their correspondence and autobiographies, do not normally talk like that, though they are liable to do so when cornered by a Socratic cross-examination. They talk about 'My efforts to reorganize the electoral system' and about difficulties in character drawing or orchestration. Indeed we tend to suspect that a man who protests that his aim is the production of Beauty or Goodness is something of a charlatan.

This however brings us back to an earlier question, namely, if it is granted that what an artist is trying to do is to paint a jug with sunflowers in it and what a statesman is trying to do is to change the divorce laws of a particular country, how does he or anybody else know when his efforts are successful? What evidence will justify him in saying 'The picture is a good one' or 'The reform is beneficial'?

Here it is necessary to be careful. In the sense in which a puzzle can be solved, neither the artist nor the statesman can ever be said to have achieved his aim. That, however, is not to say that he always fails, but simply that he is not solving puzzles. Collingwood has put this point very clearly as far as the artist is concerned. 'I learned what some critics and aestheticians never know to the end of their lives, that no "work of art" is ever finished, so that in that sense of the phrase there is no such thing as a "work of art" at all. Work ceases upon the picture or manuscript, not because it is finished, but because sending-in day is at hand, or because the printer is clamorous for copy, or because "I am sick of working at this thing" or "I can't see what more I can do to it".' The position of the statesman is essentially the same. Nobody can finish reforming the laws of England or even the laws of cricket; and nobody can improve on the right answer to a chess problem. This, it must be repeated, does not prejudice the fact that there are tricks to be learned and puzzles to be solved before the statesman or the artist can get on with his proper business. The point here is simply that there are no timeless or spaceless tests in matters of this kind. To suppose that there are is again to slip into the language which is appropriate to puzzle-solving. 'Once solved, always solved' is indeed good enough for bridge problems but political difficulties are not of that type. What was a good system of political institutions for the Athenians or the Romans is most unlikely to be a good one for the Russians or the Indonesians. This perhaps suggests that statesmen as well as artists, philosophers, historians, and scientific researchers are all completely beyond the reach of rational appraisal, but this is by no means the case. In the first place, every man appraises his own work, in the second place his colleagues in the same field of activity appraise it, and finally there are expert critics whose job it is to criticize and approve or disapprove of it both when it is first achieved and after he is dead.

These appraisals differ from one another and they are complementary. The agent himself usually knows better than anyone else can know what are the specific difficulties which he needs to overcome. In so far as these depend on his own character he normally has opportunities which other people do not have for estimating them. He feels what other people can only guess or infer that he feels. But his judgement is not infallible or incorrigible. Contemporaries may see clearly that he exaggerates some difficulties and underrates others, they may know some facts or some technical tricks which he does not know, though it would not be impossible for him to learn them. Experts, whether contemporary or subsequent, are again in a different position. They know less about the agent's personality and facilities for finding out relevant facts and techniques, but they know many things which the agent did not know and frequently could not have known. Augustus might have acted differently if he had been familiar with the works of Einstein, Keynes, and Freud.

All the same it is a mistake to suppose that these types of appraisal exclude one another. It is rather the case that none of them can be carried out effectively without reference to the others. We should hesitate to call a man a great statesman or a great artist if we knew that he completely ignored all criticism, however well informed, and criticism as well as history fails if it takes no account of the feelings, difficulties, and limitations of the people with whom it is concerned.

Now just as there are experts whose profession it is to pass judgement on pictures and symphonies, so there are specialists in political institutions. Their function is very similar to that of selection committees in that they have both to predict the probable consequences of political actions and to express a view as to the suitability of such actions at a particular time and place. They cannot determine whether or not proportional representation is a good institution in the abstract; nor can anyone else, since 'Is proportional representation a good institution?' is not a difficult but an empty question. But they can have a reasoned view as to whether it would be wise to introduce it in Great Britain or the U.S.S.R. or the Gold Coast in 1953. They can also give reasons for maintaining that some institutions such as slavery or censorship which actually exist in some associations are good or bad in the context in which they are found. Certainly such judgements are always the judgement of individuals. What else could they be? Certainly they are subject to error, that is, they may be rejected without logical contradiction by a majority of equally well-informed and impartial individuals, or by more intelligent or better informed successors. This however is only to say that they are empirical judgements and not deductions from axioms within a postulational system.

Critics are consultants. It is statesmen and not consultants who make decisions. Consultants can exercise a substantial influence over statesmen, just as art critics can over artists; indeed an important test of statesmanship is the intelligent use of consultants. Rulers should not be overawed by them as experts and should not ignore their recommendations in favour of amateurish intuitions. In fact, however, the gap between statesman and consultant or that between artist and critic is not so wide as exposition makes it appear. Statesmen in the end have to do their own appraising and critics who are wholly incompetent at doing what they appraise are seldom of much use.

By this time I may have given the impression that I am trying to answer the familiar question 'Is politics (or statesmanship) an art or a science?' and am maintaining that it is an art. This impression is mistaken as I shall now show. There are differences between the activities of statesmen and those of artists which must be emphasized if confusion is to be avoided.

In the first place, the activities of statesmen are not confined to reforming political institutions. We do not call a man a statesman if he has concentrated so much on improving the national arrangements for social security that he has lost a war or precipitated a revolution. The position of artists is quite different. Admittedly there have been periods and groups of people who have held that the artist's primary function is not to paint sunflowers but to teach moral lessons, but this is merely a failure to distinguish art from advertisement.

Connected with this is the further point that the artist is to a far greater extent the final judge of his own achievement than the statesman ever can be. It is not an adverse criticism of an artist to say that he was too far ahead of his times to be appreciated by his contemporaries. Statesmen on the other hand are doomed to failure unless at least a considerable number of their contemporaries appreciate what they are trying to do. Prophets and visionaries may have great influence for good or bad, but the difference between them and statesmen needs no emphasis.

Again, statesmen, in so far as they are concerned with promoting or reforming institutions, are dealing with rules in accordance with which human beings are to behave. Artists are not. Artists cannot be cruel or selfish to their pigments or their bassoons though they may be to their wives or to the members of their orchestra. They do not, except by a metaphor, torture their instruments or coerce their canvasses. They may impose rules on themselves or their families, but their materials are subject to laws of nature and not to rules. As I said earlier when discussing puzzles and difficulties, it is possible to treat human beings as materials, but, if that is done, 'statesman' has no place in our vocabulary. We should give it up and talk instead of technicians and engineers.

The two questions which concern us as to the nature of political appraisals may now be answered. (1) It is not the case that political institutions can always or usually be completely appraised in the language of means and ends. This, however, does not make them exceptional since the same characteristic is found in aesthetic creation. It is, however, a mistake to describe the statesman as a kind of artist since this obscures the fact that statesmen deal with human beings. Flecker's *Hassan* and Machiavelli's *Prince* provide good instances of what tends to happen when this distinction is forgotten or ignored. (2) Appraisals are empirical judgements made by individuals. We go wrong if we try to assimilate them to deductive conclusions from axioms. You may always disagree with my appraisals but it is an abuse of language to say that appraisals are simply statements of baseless prejudices. This can be shown by asking whether 'unprejudiced report' is a significant phrase or not. If it is not, 'prejudiced' is a useless word. If it is, there is no reason why appraisals should be more prejudiced than statements about shapes or sizes. The illusion here arises because most of us have been trained to talk as if there were a Grand Appraiser who knows all the right answers and to whose Appraisals we try to approach. But those who use this or similar language do not explain what it means. If appraisals are empirical judgements, 'infallible appraisal' and 'incorrigible appraisal' are contradictions. But what would a non-empirical appraisal be like?

But what is to be done when disagreements occur?

Fortunately we are not destitute of resources. I can draw your attention to points you may have missed, and we can both study the works of professionals and improve our knowledge of the actual situation by the ordinary methods of research. Certainly there are limits to this process, but it is not nearly as barren or unprofitable as it is often supposed to be.

All this is straightforward enough, indeed it is rather elementary; for the activity under consideration is one with which we are all perfectly familiar. It appears to be complicated and inexplicable only if we misunderstand the place and function of *a priori* or mathematical thinking in our explanations of what happens in the world. It is true that Aristotle did much to correct the mistaken view of Plato that important discoveries could be made about human conduct and human institutions by means of pure thought divorced from observation. Aristotle and his school were careful and industrious students of comparative political institutions, though the varieties which they were in a position to analyse were not very great. In spite of this the belief that some factual knowledge could be gained by analysing and defining political words persisted, and this is not very surprising. It was comforting to believe in the existence of an immutable, non-empirical world which could be explored by the methods of geometry and mathematics and to maintain that the models constructed on these principles were reliable guides for statesmen; and it was much less exhausting to enunciate solemnities about the State, the Individual, Rights, and Liberty than it would have been to analyse and appraise the actual institutions of the British, the Russians, or the Americans. Short cuts are often popular but seldom short, and this one has proved to be a failure; but, largely as a result of the medieval illusion that the Empire was a very special kind of institution and that monarchs were somehow different from ordinary human beings, the belief that enquiries into the foundations of politics could achieve valuable results has persisted.

But if there really are no political foundations to be discovered, is political philosophy nothing more than a delusion? In one sense it is, and so are the philosophy of art, the philosophy of biology, and the philosophy of physics. There are no meta-worlds waiting to be explored and to yield their secrets when they are at last visited by intrepid metaphysicians. This however is a verbal point. Whether we decide to retain the phrase 'political philosophy' or not, a great deal needs to be done about the language in which discussions of political institutions are conducted. It would be uneconomical to require those whose job it is to investigate, describe, and appraise political institutions to exercise perpetual vigilance over their own linguistic usages. Yet the language of politics like the language involved in any other serious study inevitably exercises a certain constraint over its users. This is more clearly true of the sciences in which avowedly technical usage predominates; it is more dangerous where ordinary words are normally used in special or slightly unconventional ways. It is here that the greatest care is needed to keep factual difficulties and linguistic conventions distinct from one another, and this cannot be done once and for all because of modifications of usage which we generally do not notice while they are happening and often do not notice or clearly recognize after they have happened. The most important service the Marxists have rendered to philosophical thought about political institutions is to compel us to pay attention to some of these modifications and to attempt to analyse them correctly.

It is important, too, to work through the competing ideologies and to see them in their proper perspective. Until this is done they tend to confuse and distort political thinking and to make us forget that governing at any level is essentially a matter of judgement and decision by statesmen and rulers and not a matter of theoretical reasoning. Whenever this is forgotten, there is a strong tendency to relapse into a foolish kind of political fatalism. This is clearly encouraged by the Marxist and organic myths, since both explicitly require nobody except possibly a small body of the elect to make any careful study of political institutions. It is common ground to both of them that an ideal set of institutions for human beings as such can be achieved, and that when it has been achieved there is nothing more to be done. Humanity can then sit back and take a rest. There will be no further improvements to be made; it would be impious to suggest that there might be.

The traditional democratic theory looks different and has a more progressive ring about it, but the difference is not as great as it appears to be. As developed by the philosophical radicals and the constitutional lawyers of the early nineteenth century, the theory assumes that human political behaviour is an inevitable product of a few simple psychological 'laws', and that there are thrusts and pushes which economists discover and which produce accurately predictable consequences. These consequences are generally beneficial to humanity. They become damaging, like the force of gravity or the tides, unless steps are taken to see that the ignorant and superstitious do not try to oppose or interfere with them. So again in the end it seems that nobody will need to do anything. Politics is highly intelligent non-interference.

This attitude of resignation is well suited to the convention according to which the word 'law' has only one meaning so that in politics as well as in chemistry and physics laws are not made but discovered; and the opposed Idealist doctrine according to which laws are not discovered but made in physics as in politics is only superficially different. For that which does the making is not the individual man but is Reason or Mind, and it comes to the same thing if we say instead 'Nature' or 'God'. I believe that this is the dangerous feature about all the ideologies. They do not logically necessitate passivity in politics, since they do not logically necessitate anything, but they have considerable psychological force in the direction of leaving things alone for the benefit of any ruling class. 'Classes are abolished in the U.S.S.R., so no further political change is needed there', 'The Real is the Rational; the Rational is the Real', '*Laissez faire*' can all be profitably employed to discourage and if necessary to repress critical appraisals of existing institutions.

But if we refuse to be dominated by them and understand their position the ideologies have their uses too. All of them have some sort of vague empirical appraisal as their origin. The empirical truth which is abstractly and misleadingly stated by Hegel is that some associations are important and that we should think at least twice before we set ourselves to disintegrate them. The early democrats recognized equally clearly that individuals are important and should not be maltreated or repressed without good reason. Marx saw that existing institutions can be changed if individuals have sufficient initiative and courage to change them. Hence, if we take the ideologies for what they are, namely formal rules for the guidance of legislators based on inductive generalizations, they are often useful guides to appraisal and action. So are the standard rules recommended by games coaches and art critics. The coaches and critics, if they are competent, are not themselves dominated by these precepts and do not expect or desire that other people should be dominated by them. They are making recommendations for conduct, not proposing definitions or linguistic conventions.

One further point in favour of ideologies is worth making. Our appraisals are empirical, hence they are not incorrigible. We can make mistakes about what is important as we can about anything else. It is easy to overlook this and to insist dogmatically on the truth of judgements which have been formulated after a very casual and incomplete study of the facts. Abstract generalizations about natural rights or class warfare will not prevent this and are in themselves of no assistance in the refutation of mistaken judgements. But they have at least the restricted use of suggesting to us that we may possibly be mistaken and encouraging us to think again.

§4. *Conclusion*

Appraisals of the goodness and badness of political institutions are like all other appraisals in that they are formulated by individuals. They vary because individuals are sometimes biassed, short-sighted, selfish, unintelligent and so on. And since it requires much care and training to overcome such limitations it is not surprising that the variations which we find in these departments are greater than those which occur in weighing, counting, and measuring, which are a great deal easier to accomplish. What has to be remembered is that a personal view is not necessarily biassed or dishonest. Indeed there is no more in this than the simple but important truth that people can be educated, and being educated is not the same thing as learning how to do puzzles successfully. Education is not a kind of psychological conditioning, neither is it complete intellectual *laissez-faire*. To say that anyone is educated is at least to say that his thinking is sufficiently disciplined and his knowledge of human beings is sufficiently extensive to qualify him to pass judgement on some types of human association. 'Educated' does not mean the same as 'literate' or 'learned' or 'clever'.

Now it is clear that 'Is the British legal system a good institution?', 'Is it superior to that of the U.S.S.R.?' are not philosophical questions. Almost everyone would admit that we cannot even begin to answer them without a prolonged study of the way in which the two systems work both in theory and in practice. 'Is communism superior to democracy?' looks easier but in fact it is not. Obviously all of us have not the time or the opportunity to go into such questions in detail, yet we cannot avoid taking sides, so what is to be done? In fact the situation is not alarming. Each of us has his own tests, which are no doubt rough and crude, but they will serve their purpose, which is to check and confirm the conclusions of experts based on thorough research. My own are approximately as follows:

1. Does the political system under consideration censor the reading of those who are subject to it and impose restrictions on teaching?
2. Does it maintain that any political or other principles are immutable and therefore beyond criticism?
3. Does it impose restrictions on the intercourse of its members with those who live under different systems?

These are not final or conclusive tests, nor are they the only ones that matter, but any set of institutions which includes all these restrictions is *prima facie* a bad one, and the reason for claiming that it is bad is the presumption that those who are subject to it would reject it or escape from it if the restrictions were removed. I would therefore add:

4. Do the rulers of the association which has these institutions find most of their supporters among the illiterate, the uneducated, and the superstitious?

It does not follow that institutions which successfully pass all these tests are good. The absence of restrictions does not guarantee anything. But it seems to me important that people should make correct appraisals and it is certain that they cannot do this if they are kept in ignorance of the facts. I must repeat however that this is my personal view, or prejudice if that word is preferred. It has nothing philosophical about it and may be rejected by anyone who disapproves of it. I suggest, however, that anyone who does reject it should offer an alternative and at least equally usable set of tests. To put the matter shortly in the much-criticized but perfectly correct words of J. S. Mill, 'The only proof capable of being given that an object is visible, is that people actually see it. The only proof that a sound is audible, is that people hear it: and so of the other sources of our experience. In like manner, I apprehend, the sole evidence it is possible to produce that anything is desirable, is that people do actually desire it'.

We may now consider a further question, namely, 'In what sort of circumstances is it legitimate to interfere with the political institutions of other people?' This again is a question about education. We may have reasons for believing that a particular system is retained only because of the ignorance and inexperience of those who live under it. This, however, does not by itself justify any policy of action or inaction. The belief that either the one or the other must always be right is simply a product of the mistaken disjunction which I am criticizing. It originates in the false dilemma between subjective and objective judgements which encourages us to say either: (a) it is always unjustifiable to interfere with other people since all that is involved is a matter of personal preference and 'right' and 'wrong' are meaningless in this context, or: (b) I have a special source of information which gives me infallible information as to what will be beneficial for other people; and if they do not know what is good for them it is my duty to improve them and 'force them to be free'. Both these assertions are instances of the type of generalization which is purely formal and empty as it stands but which can easily be interpreted in such a way as to lend apparent support to disreputable commissions and omissions.

The reason why it is difficult in concrete cases to decide between intervention and non-intervention is that we are seldom or never quite sure of what the results of our action or inaction will be. 'Results' here is open to a possible misunderstanding since it suggests that we are concerned with the selection of means to a pre-determined end. This is seldom the case except in a special sense of 'end'. We use 'result', 'consequence', and 'effect' both when we are talking about an achievement of which it makes no sense to ask how long it took to happen and of a process which takes time and may happen quickly or slowly. Thus it is correct to say 'The result of the match was a draw' and also 'The result of the Government's full employment policy is progressive inflation of the currency'; or, combining both uses, 'The result of his fall was that he broke his leg and was lame for some months'. It is almost always in the second of these senses that we talk of the results of political reforms, and that is why, even if we are well-informed about the relevant facts, we find it difficult or impossible to predict their results with any precision. They do not have a one-track, specifiable line of consequences culminating in a win or a loss as moves in chess or leads in bridge tend to have, and therefore we often cannot have the evidence for framing a series of hypothetical statements on which convincing appraisals can be based.

Occasionally it looks as if a really good electronic computer would do the business for us, but this is very seldom true. As in the case of works of art, it usually makes no sense to say that the reform of a system of political institutions has been completed, though it makes perfect sense to say that the system has been improved. Hence it is possible for us to differ in the same sort of way as that in which selection committees differ as to the relative importance of different factors in an agreed result; and there is much more scope for disagreement in political matters because human beings differ considerably in the importance they attach to long-term as distinct from short-term consequences. I think it could easily be shown that the average intelligent American is much more impatient than the average intelligent Russian; and this makes it difficult for Americans and Russians to work out a policy which both regard as sensible, though it is difficult to see how fighting about it would help matters.

In fact the crucial question which needs to be answered before we set out to reform other peoples' institutions is not 'What are the best institutions for human beings to live under?' but 'Do we know enough about the facts to be qualified to give helpful advice in this case?', and it should be remembered that the relevant facts include the traditions, history, geographical conditions, education, and customary standard of living of the people concerned. It is a very much more complicated and difficult matter than the revision of the betting laws or even the divorce laws in Great Britain or the United States, and these are quite complicated and difficult enough. It is therefore rather surprising that the complete reform of the institutions of the U.S.S.R. or the Indians or the Chinese are subjects on which so many people are prepared to offer advice without any qualifications whatever, though few baseball players would consider themselves competent to act as expert advisers for revising the rules of cricket.

Nevertheless anyone who has the requisite experience and knowledge can sometimes give useful advice as to political institutions and it is sometimes justifiable to bring pressure to bear on other people to follow it. There are no certified general rules or principles which will enable us to say dogmatically which these occasions are or how much pressure is legitimate, but there are rough inductive generalizations which are helpful. Good colonial administrators are perhaps the people best qualified to formulate these.

I do not see what grounds there are for expecting or claiming any greater degree of certainty than this. If we lack judgement in such matters or have inadequate information, we shall probably get the answers wrong, though 'wrong' here does not mean what it means when we are talking about arithmetic or crossword puzzles, for there is no demonstrably right answer. Hence there is no ideal set of institutions, though it is still significant for anybody to maintain that one system is better than another and that any system admits of being improved. It must be allowed however that comparisons have little significance where associations of people at very different levels of intellectual, political, and cultural development are concerned, and it is at least permissible to enquire whether the inhabitants of the U.S.S.R. and those of Western Europe and the U.S.A. are sufficiently alike to make comparisons between their institutions a valuable undertaking. Is it not rather like attempting to compare Bach's B Minor Mass with Wagner's 'Ring', and is not this a futile proceeding?

However this may be, it seems clear to me that *a priori* principles have as much and as little use in making political decisions and political appraisals as they have in fighting battles or criticizing works of art. They save time and trouble and sometimes help us to avoid elementary mistakes, but they cannot make our decisions or do our appraising for us.

CHAPTER 6

Politics and Morals

'GOOD' in contemporary English usage is an unsatisfactory
word. This is not because we use it in a vague or imprecise
way. Most of the words we make use of in ordinary discourse have this characteristic and are none the worse for it.
Nor does it matter that the things, people, acts, and situations to which it is applied vary from time to time and from
place to place. Only a little care and thought is necessary
to avoid confusion arising from either of these causes. What
is genuinely troublesome is that 'good' is used as a sort of
utility word for favourable appraisals of entities which are
of different logical types, and this encourages subjectivist
mistakes. For since 'Jones is a good tennis player', 'Smith
is a good man', 'Britain has a good legal system', and
'*Hamlet* is a good tragedy' all give different kinds of information, it is easy to suppose that, since 'good' occurs
in all of them, it must refer to the psychological state of
the speaker and not to the things he is speaking about.

I cannot deal adequately with this subject here. It
requires a book to itself. It might therefore seem advisable
to say no more about it than I have already done in connexion with subjectivism and objectivism in political
appraisals. But to leave the matter there might look like an
evasion of some familiar questions. Thus it seems proper to
ask 'Do political appraisals express or derive from moral
judgements or attitudes?' 'Are statesmen subject to the
same moral rules as ordinary men?' and 'Is a good man
always a good citizen?'. And finally there is Hume's com-
plaint. 'In every system of morality which I have hitherto
met with, I have always remarked, that the author proceeds
for some time in the ordinary way of reasoning, and estab-
lishes the being of a God, or makes some observations concerning human affairs; when of a sudden I am surprised to

find that instead of the usual copulations of propositions, *is*, and *is not*, I meet with no proposition that is not connected with an *ought*, or an *ought not*. This change is imperceptible; but is, however, of the last consequence. For as this *ought*, or *ought not*, expresses some new relation or affirmation, it is necessary that it should be observed and explained; and at the same time, that a reason should be given, for what seems altogether inconceivable, how this new relation can be a deduction from others, which are entirely different from it.' All these demand some elucidation of 'good' and therefore I cannot avoid further discussion of it.

The most important error which has to be avoided is one which originated from a great over-simplification to which traditional logic and metaphysics lent considerable support. For a long time it was tacitly agreed that all descriptive words referred either to substances or to qualities or to relations. Other parts of speech like verbs and adverbs which did not fit this scheme had to be replaced by words which did fit it before they could be recognized as respectable for purposes of logical discourse. Now on the face of it 'good' does not stand for a substance or a relation; hence it has to stand for a quality. There is no meaning in 'There is a piece of good in the larder' which would make 'good' like 'cheese' or in 'William is the good of Richard' which would make it like 'father'. But 'This beer is good' is superficially very much like 'This beer is cold'. Yet even here the resemblance is only superficial since we test the truth of 'This beer is cold' with a metrical device called a thermometer, but no similar procedure will do in the case of 'This beer is good'. However we may persist and say 'It is true that "good" does not stand for an ordinary quality, but it must stand for a quality of some sort. Hence there must be a special kind of quality which I will call "tertiary" or "transcendental"; and there must be a special kind of observation which I shall call "intuition" by means of which the presence or absence of good in beer, actions, legal systems, tragedies, and human beings can be detected'.

This idea is not completely wrong. It is correct in that observation and judgement are not the same activity. A man may be extremely competent at one of them and a duffer at the other. What is mistaken is the doctrine that to appraise is to recognize the presence or absence of a quality at all.

The second point to notice is this. We may be asked, 'If not a quality, then what?', and it is essential to insist that there is no one simple answer to this question. All the statements I have given as instances are of different types and each of them requires separate treatment. There are, however, two general points which can usefully be made as a preliminary to more detailed discussion. The first concerns aesthetic criticisms. It is a curious fact that modern English has no general word which can be used without embarrassment to express favourable aesthetic appraisal. 'Beautiful' has practically dropped out of use except in descriptions of scenery in Guide Books and the advertisements issued by travel agencies. 'Pretty' is derogatory and 'admirable' patronizing. None of these can be used to describe the symphonies of Brahms or the tragedies of Shakespeare. 'Sublime' now sounds pompous, and 'excellent' and 'first class' belong to examiners. So we are reduced to saying 'very good' or possibly 'great'.

I do not pretend to explain this linguistic austerity. It is just a fact which we must accept as far as ordinary language is concerned. But it is philosophically tiresome because it lends colour to the supposition that all appraisal statements give the same kind of information and that this information is not about whatever it is that is being appraised. It is therefore convenient to use 'beautiful' in the present context. This leads to the second general point which needs to be made here. Works of art do not act. We may indeed describe a picture or a symphony as 'moving', 'frightening', 'depressing', and so on, and such words, if they are correctly applied, tell the hearer that most people who see or listen to the work in question feel frightened, or cheerful, or angry, as the case may be. But I think it would be generally agreed that a critic may experience none of these feelings and yet may make a sound appraisal of the beauty of what he is criticizing. Many would maintain that he is more likely to do so if he is not moved to fury, misery, or any other feeling by it. To put it differently, being beautiful is not a disposition like being brittle or being soluble, though it is true that seeing and hearing things which are beautiful is often the cause of emotion in observers. Indeed 'That is beautiful' is more like 'That is yellow' than it is like 'That is brittle'. There are important differences but I do not propose to go into them here.

Now as we have already seen there is a considerable resemblance between appraisals of institutions and appraisals of works of art. Some differences have already been mentioned. Among these must now be included the fact that dispositional characteristics are of great importance in institutions. We describe them as 'flexible', 'convenient', 'inequitable', 'adaptable', and so on. Now we do not here imply that they occasion any kind of sentiment or feeling in spectators; we mean rather that it is possible for people who adopt them to act in roughly specifiable ways without breaking the rules; for instance, they can change their government or obtain reforms without organizing revolutions. Flexibility, whether we praise or blame it, is a dispositional characteristic.

We can now consider in rather more detail the use of 'good' in moral as well as in political appraisals. Let us however begin with something more simple than these. Take 'This half-crown is good'. We may contradict this either by saying, 'No, it is a bad one', or 'It is not a half-crown but a forgery'. Suppose, however, that we accept it as true, we are committing ourselves to two sets of assertions, the one wholly categorical or metrical, the other conditional. Thus we are maintaining (1) that the coin was fabricated at the Mint and that it satisfies the current legal standards of shape, size, weight, and purity, (2) that it is legal tender, that is, that we could buy any of a variety of goods or services with it if we chose to do so.

It is important to notice that both kinds of information are conveyed by our ordinary use of 'good', but that, when we are talking about actions and characters, the second is very much more prominent than the first.

We have already seen something of this in discussing the simple appraisals we habitually make when discussing games and similar activities. 'Jones is a good cricketer' or 'a good shot' are partly statements about actual achievements which can be metrically or statistically verified. They are also, and more fundamentally, statements about probable future behaviour under conditional circumstances, and the metrical data are less relevant in themselves than as evidence for or against the probability of such behaviour. 'Jones is a good citizen', or 'a good Freemason', or a good member of any institution, can be almost but not quite completely analysed on the same lines. They tell us that he has paid his subscriptions (or taxes) regularly and in full, that he has attended meetings, used his vote, kept the rules, and so on; but here again there is a large and indeed a predominant hypothetical element, 'He would defend the association if it were threatened', 'He would make sacrifices for it if required' and so on. If we ask 'Why would he do that?' 'What reason would he have for such conduct?', the only answer is 'Because he considers it a good association', and this 'good' is the quasi-aesthetic use mentioned above. There is no further move to be made. Should the answer be 'Because he expects to make a financial profit by it', we should say 'Then he is not genuinely a good citizen, he is not really a good member of that association', though his conduct may perfectly well exemplify loyalty to some other association, his family for instance or his Trade Union. There is, however, something defective about this analysis. What it is becomes more clear when we consider the further question, namely, what information is conveyed by 'Jones is a good man'? If you were to receive a testimonial to Mr Jones containing this statement and no more, you would feel that it was somewhat obscure. It might mean that he was well-qualified for the post he was seeking; again it might refer to his piety or his charitable propensities. Anyhow, it is too vague to be of any assistance. Now suppose that you are giving and not receiving a testimonial to Mr Jones and that you say of him 'He is intelligent, industrious, and trustworthy. He is also a competent athlete and can speak and read French and German'. If in reply you are asked 'Is he also a good man?' you are again in something of a quandary. Does the prospective employer want to be told that Jones is a regular churchgoer, that he is faithful to his wife, that he does not gamble and is not a Communist? Or what? The question is no doubt extremely vague but it is not without significance. To understand it we need to remember that in any association and for that matter in any game there are numerous practices which are generally approved or discouraged though nothing is said about them in the printed rules. Sometimes indeed something is said. There may be a final paragraph on 'the ethics of Bridge' or 'the traditions of the School.' There may also be more or less clearly defined and severe penalties for breaches of such rules, and these may be enforced either by public opinion or by recognized arbiters of some kind. Rules of this type do not seem to differ in any important respect from any other rules of conduct, and a disposition to act in accordance with them is just like a disposition to keep any other set of rules, whether they are adopted by the agent to control his own behaviour or imposed on him by some other authority. Moral rules dealing with sexual conduct, religious observances, usury, and the care of children can be just as detailed and just as strictly enforced as any other kind of rule. Anyone who doubts this should study the early history of the New England Colonies.

In fact the distinction between moral and political rules is not logical, it is almost entirely religious in origin and character. In countries where one religion is completely dominant it hardly exists. In others where it is agreed that political rules are made by popularly elected representatives and are to be justified solely by empirical reasons, it is often the case that moral rules are still supposed to have some other justification and to be the special preserve of the priests. It is difficult to see how this can be more than a stage of transition or, as some would prefer to call it, a temporary aberration. For there is just no possibility of distinguishing for practical purposes between the two spheres. The British Education Acts reveal this clearly enough. They also show that it is possible, at any rate for a time, to invent a practical compromise which will work, although the distinction on which it is supposed to rest is non-existent.

This is not the end of the matter. It is well known that a man may keep all the rules laid down by the priests as well as those laid down by the politicians and still be regarded as a bad, or at any rate, an unsatisfactory character; and this suggests that there is yet another rule or set of rules which has to be considered. 'Do as you would be done by' and 'Treat human beings always as ends and never merely as means' may be cited as attempts to formulate such a rule. But it is a logical mistake to suppose that we are here dealing with a rule at all. It is not a question of following an extra prescription, but one of following recognized prescriptions in a special way.

What is meant can perhaps be shown by reference to what was said earlier about good statesmen, good citizens, and good Trade Unionists. One may say for instance that Mussolini before 1940 did everything which a good statesman would have done, yet he was not a good statesman at all but a political adventurer. The point here would be that he had no interest in the Italians except as pieces in a game he was playing. In the same way Hobbes was convinced that his monarch would always act in such a way as to promote the interests of his subjects, though he cared nothing for them. What this comes to is simply that any possible rule can be kept selfishly or disinterestedly and that to do acts which look unselfish is not the same as to act unselfishly. Certainly this kind of conduct which is what in ordinary speech we describe as 'really' or 'genuinely moral' is the realization of a disposition, but this disposition is a sort of second order disposition. It is not under the agent's control even to the extent that other dispositions are. An ambitious man may make it his policy to curb his ambition; a selfish man may make it his policy to give liberally to charitable objects, but it makes no sense to say that he may make it his policy to act unselfishly. Hence unselfishness, though it is not untestable, is not testable as easily or in the same way as other dispositions, nor can one reach the same degree of certainty about it as one can about them. Provided that these distinctions are remembered it matters very little how we choose to use the phrases 'a good man' and 'a morally good man'. In the light of them it is possible to see fairly clearly how the questions concerning political and moral appraisals with which this Chapter began can be answered.

'Do political appraisals express moral attitudes?' is badly put. It suggests the mistaken belief that there are two distinguishable spheres called 'morals' and 'politics' with the implication that some actions fall into one of these and others into the other and also that the actions which are described as 'moral' are invariably more important than those which are described as 'political'. All this is very misleading and is liable to cause unnecessary confusion. Certainly the rules made up by politicians are not the only rules we recognize, and among the non-political rules there is an important group usually called 'moral' which comprises (a) formalized rules laid down by religious authorities, (b) conventions recognized by groups of people who may be, but need not be, organized in definite associations. Social groups normally have such conventions which resemble closely the codes of behaviour accepted by professional men like lawyers and doctors. In so far as such groups are politically influential, it is to be expected that they will attempt (and to a greater or less extent will be successful) to getting their codes written into the laws of the State. In this sense it is correct to say that political rules are derived from moral rules, though it would be more accurate to say that the codes of behaviour which influential minorities make for themselves tend to be enforced by law on majorities for whose use they may or may not be suitable. In States which adopt representative institutions, the reverse process also can be observed, that is to say, the conventions which the majority find convenient may be enforced by law on influential minorities; for technical reasons this is much less common.

In the second and more important sense of 'moral', moral conduct is not a matter of obeying rules, and therefore it is useless to say that political rules depend on moral rules. But it is true that people who tend to act in an unselfish or impartial way are likely to support humanitarian or inoffensive measures both in political legislation and in conventional codes of behaviour. In other words morality in this sense has a definite though seldom a decisive influence both on morality in the other sense and on the explicit rules of association of all kinds. This is not a precise statement, but the matter under consideration is not one which admits of precise treatment. 'Are statesmen subject to the same moral rules as ordinary men?' is another unclear question. It can be more or less elucidated as follows. Statesmen are in very much the same position as the heads or representatives of other associations, headmasters, Trade Union leaders, and heads of Government departments. They represent or speak for the members of their associations, and it is their function to look after the interests of those members. The difference between statesmen and other leaders is that the relations between associations other than States are by now largely formalized, regulated by law and subject to State control. Relations between States, on the other hand, are only beginning to be formalized in international law. Hence the degree to which it is proper to exercise force or pressure of any kind on the members or representatives of other associations for the benefit of members of one's own association is still mostly a matter of judgement which has to be exercised in the normal way. Most people would now consider that Bismarck, for instance, paid too little attention to the interests of non-Prussians; but at the other end of the scale it is possible to underrate the importance of members of the association for which one is speaking. Some would say that British statesmen have erred in this direction since 1945. There is, however, no recognized rule on the subject. It is fair to say that there are some standards of international behaviour which are generally recognized; but their influence is never conclusive and becomes negligible when national survival is or is believed to be at stake. Their force however is sufficient to make most statesmen unwilling to break them openly. Thus the distinction between 'statesman' and 'ordinary man' is almost wholly artificial. Anybody who represents any association may act tyrannically or feebly towards members of other associations; and there is no rule of thumb method for deciding when he is doing either. It is a matter of degree and therefore the search for hard and fast distinctions is unprofitable.

This discussion really covers the similar distinction between 'good man' and 'good citizen'. This depends partly on the existence of different associations with their own rules and conventions which are liable to be incompatible as in the case of Church and State, and partly on the distinction between the keeping of rules and the spirit in which they are kept. Again no general answer can be given to 'Can a bad man be a good citizen?' It depends on the way in which the question is understood.

Finally there is the question which Hume formulated so bluntly and which reappears in later controversies between naturalistic and non-naturalistic writers on morals. It may be put in a slightly different way as 'What is the distinction between descriptive and normative statements, between

"This is the case" and "This ought to be the case"?' Hume's method of expressing it in the language of bridge-building is about as misleading as it can be. It shows clearly enough that there can be no legitimate inference from 'is' to 'ought to be', but it leaves the impression that this is an awkward and embarrassing truth. To say 'There is no bridge here' at least encourages the belief that there might be a bridge if anyone had the money and the enterprise to build one. Yet this clearly will not do at all. When we say 'You ought not to do that' we are using the language of rules, and it is grammatically impossible to infer a rule from any set of facts. Rules as we have already seen are prescriptions. They are not like natural laws. We make them up. We do not find or discover them except in the sense that we read them in books or legal codes. We may guess what the rules of England or the rules of cricket are by observing the behaviour of Englishmen and cricketers, but that is an entirely different matter from making the 'laws' of England or the 'laws' of cricket.

Again as a piece of grammar, rules are either kept or broken. They cannot logically be more or less broken. The number of British subjects who infringe the currency regulations every year is a matter of statistical assessment, but each individual either keeps or infringes them on any given occasion. Fundamentally 'ought' is a legal word. When it is used with any care and precision we may fairly assume that we are concerned with hard and fast disjunctions, for what is required is always a decision. To say that someone has half decided to do something is to say that he has not decided but is quite likely to do so. In more technical language, decisions are achievements, not performances.

Strictly speaking 'X ought to do Y' always refers to a rule of some sort, and there are many different kinds of rule. But 'ought' suffers from the same sort of confusion as 'moral' does. Statements in which it occurs can usually be analysed in terms of a rule or rules, but sometimes this will not do. For in ordinary speech 'You ought to do that',

'This ought to be the case' refer to consequences and mean simply 'It would be better if . . .' They concern appraisals which may or may not involve the keeping of rules. Thus 'The Russians ought to have representative institutions', 'The British ought to have proportional representation' are unclear statements. They might have reference to an actual system of world government with formalized rules and clearly defined sanctions, or they might have reference to an actual body of universal opinion which accepted these as rules and imposed more or less effective penalties for disobedience. More usually, however, they are straightforward appraisals. In that case the language of disjunctions is inappropriate. We need 'more' and 'less' rather than 'either . . . or' to describe the situation. Thus while it is correct to say that if we knew all the probable consequences of our acts, we should very seldom be in any doubt as to what we ought to do, this is not the same as to say that if we knew all the political and other rules, we should always know what we ought to do. The most intricate knowledge of the rules of golf will not tell us how to get out of a bunker; quite ordinary knowledge of them will tell us that we are not permitted to throw the ball on to the fairway. Thus Hume's question is not a genuine question at all. In one sense of 'ought' there is no bridge from 'is' to 'ought to be', and it makes no sense to say that there might be; in the other, though bridge-building is a most unhappy metaphor, it is perfectly correct to say that only by intensive study of the facts can we reach sound appraisals and advise other people as to their best course of action.

The purpose of this Chapter is entirely therapeutic. It is intended to show that when verbal confusions are tidied up most of the questions of traditional political philosophy are not unanswerable. All of them are confused formulations of purely empirical difficulties. This does not mean that these are themselves easy to deal with, but it does mean that writers on political institutions and statesmen, not philosophers, are the proper people to deal with them. As empirical questions they do have answers, but the answers are neither simple nor demonstrably and incorrigibly true, nor can they be discovered by any process of non-empirical intuition. What we need to get us out of our political difficulties is a good deal more thought and a good deal less emotion than is usually devoted to them.

INDEX

Absolute standards, 20, 30–3, 61, 94
Abstractions, 102, 103
Acheson, Dean, 85
Agrippa, Menenius, 104
Alice in Wonderland, quoted, 63
Appearance, 105
Appraisal, 13, 14, 15, 43, 182–5
  German terms, 42, 43
Aristocracy, 10
Aristophanes, 145
Aristotle, 10, 36, 38, 77, 105, 121, 139, 171
Associations, human, 12, 13, 18, 45, 66, 73, 74, 80, 92, 103, 104
Associations, 48, 49, 53, 54, 80, 95, 113–17, 133, 189, 190
Athens, 33, 52, 68, 84
Atomists, 116–17
Austin, 52
'Authority', meaning of, 50–6
  origins of, 51, 52, 53

Berkeley, 89
Black markets, 67
Bolshevist Revolution (1917), 49
Bolshevists, 126
Bosanquet, 110
Bradley, 85, 110
Burke, 102, 103, 110
Butler, Bishop, 89
Bye-laws, 98

Calculi, 41–2
Cambridge University, 84
Capitalism, 10, 71, 72, 79, 86, 101, 129, 132
China, 86
Chronometers, 31
Church, relation to the State, 10

Cicero, 46
Civil Society, 101, 110, 112
Classical political philosophy, 36ff.
Classical writers, 10, 15, 48
Codified laws, 59
Communism, 11, 19, 44, 71, 84, 87, 117ff.
Communist Manifesto, quoted, 37
  Party, 49
Communities, 49–50, 120
Compact of Society, 95, 96
Companies, limited liability, 26
Conduct, rules of, 64
Conventions, 54, 92
Croce, 85, 110

Darwin, 65
Declaration of Independence, 88
Definitions, 23, 42
Democracy, 10, 14, 44, 84ff.
  foundations of, 87–101
  metaphysics of, 97, 100, 102
Democratic theorists, 11
Descartes, 25, 78
Dialectics, 15, 105, 106, 107, 108, 109, 112, 129
Dictators, 67
Dictatorship, 10, 35
Difficulties, 75–9, 160
Disease, 80, 81

Economic planning, 82
Economic production, as controlling factor, 120
Economists, political, 89
Education, 90, 177
Einstein, 32, 41, 65
Elections, 52, 125
Electoral methods, 86
Emigration, 48

Index

Empirical politics, 94, 136, 144ff.
Engels, 121, 125, 127, 134, 135, 136
Epicurus, 116
Equality, 100, 101
Essentialist assumption, 12
Ether, 24
Euclid, 33, 34, 35, 39, 65, 67, 80, 108, 137
'Exploitation', 52, 121

Fabians, 117, 135
Fable of the Bees, 89
'Faculty of Reason', 94, 95
Fascism and Facists, 84, 87
Federal Governments, 95–6
Feudalism, 101, 130
Feuerbach, 128
Football, 98, 99
Football Association, 53, 54, 62
Force, 51, 52, 55, 56
Foundations, political, 84–143
  democratic, 87–101
  Hegelian, 101
  Marxist, 117–38
Freedom, 69–75, 91, 92, 157, 158, 159, 160
  Burke on, 102–3
  of religion, 86
  of the Press, 86
French Revolution, 102

Galileo, 31, 32, 104, 112, 148
Gallup, Dr, 66
Geneva, 33
Gentile, 110
Geometrical methods illusion of, 20, 33–36, 65
Geometry, nature of, 35
Germany, 42, 43
Gods, identification of names with, 21, 48
Government, forms of, 10, 11

Government, the, 52, 58, 59
Great Britain, 44, 48, 49, 57, 69, 84, 86, 168
  sport in, 53, 54
Greece and Greeks, 10, 17, 20, 21, 48, 84, 91, 108
Green, T. H., quoted, 37

Hegel, 10, 17, 39, 85, 87, 88, 101–5, 107–8, 110, 112, 128, 129, 131, 132, 174
Hegelian foundations, 101
Hegelian Idealism, 14, 87
Hegelians, 74, 112, 123
Herodotus, 84
History, philosophy of, 109
Hitler, Adolf, 56, 82, 87, 119, 142, 147
Hobbes, 17, 36, 39, 52, 69, 85, 121, 187
  State of Nature, 69
Home Office, 98
Human associations, 12, 13, 18, 45, 66, 73, 74, 80, 92, 103, 104
Human conduct, 66, 100
Hume, 89, 93, 145, 181–2, 190, 191

'Idea of Good', 140
Idealism, 74, 87, 136, 173
Idealists, 11
Ideals, study of, 33
Ideas, 21
  Plato on, 36
Ideologies. *See* Foundations
Illusions, philosophical, 20ff.
Immortal soul, the, 21, 104
Individual rights, 86
Industrial organization, 80
Institutions, human, 46
  non-political, 48
  political, evaluation of, 14
Intellectualism, 82
International co-operation, 81

196

Jefferson, 88, 102
Jews, 43, 82
Joint ownership, 26

Kant, Immanuel, 88, 93, 95, 96, 106, 145, 163
Kautsky, 134
Kautskyism, 126
Kepler, 112
Keynes, 79
Kulaks, 82

Labour Party, 110
Language, eccentricities of, 9
  implications of, 11, 12
  usage, 42
Law, verbal confusion concerning, 62
'Law and the Rule of Law', 61–9
Lawgivers, 67
Law of Reason, 96
Law of the Land, 67
Laws, 58
  of Athens, 68
  of England, 66, 68
  of Great Britain, 57–9
Laws of Nature, 62
Lawyers, 27, 47
Legal rights, 60
  systems, 68, 69
  terminology, 23
Legislation, 61
Legislators, 57
Lenin, 15, 123, 127, 131, 134, 135, 136, 137
Liberalism, 86
  nineteenth-century, 71
Liberty. *See* Freedom
Liechtenstein, 47
Lincoln, Abraham, 42
Lobachevsky, 39
Locke, 39, 40, 85, 102
  Second Treatise, 87

Logic, 17ff., 96, 107
  symbols in, 22
Logical analysis, 19, 116
L.C.C., 114
Lords, cricket ground, 59
Loyalty, Mabbott on, 116
Lycurgus, 142

Mabbott, J. D., 113, 115
Mach, Ernst, 136
Machiavelli, 52, 121, 139
Magical significance of names, 18
Majorities, 52, 59
Mandeville, quoted, 89
Marx, Karl, 17, 39, 52, 85, 87, 88, 90, 101, 111, 117ff., 174
Marxism, 11, 14, 46, 72, 110, 173
  foundations of, 117–38
Marxism-Leninism-Stalinism, 137
Massachusetts (U.S.A.), 96, 146
Meaning of words, 11, 12, 13, 17
Metaphysics, 20, 94
M.C.C., 53, 57, 59
Mill, John Stuart, 16, 85, 93, 176–7
  on Liberty, 87
Miracles, 65–6
Monarchs, 51, 52, 84, 91, 98
Monarchy, 10, 39, 40, 85, 86, 138
Mussolini, 87, 119, 187

Names, magical significance of, 18
National Health Service, 162, 163, 164
N.U.R., 114
Nationalization, 26
Natural laws, 65, 66
Natural rights, 15, 60, 107
Nazis, 42, 43
Negroes, 42, 77
Neo-Platonists, 105
New England, 96
Newton, Sir Isaac, 32, 65, 78, 88, 112, 125, 137

New York, 47
Nouns, significance of, 20

Obedience, 55, 56
Objective standards, 13, 14
Oligarchy, 84, 85, 86
'Opinion', 20
Opportunism, 126
Organized labour, 124
Ownership, private, 26
    public, 26, 120
Oxford University, 84

Parliaments, 10
Perceptible objects, 20
Philosopher Kings, 138–43
Philosophy, Plato's definition, 22
Philosophy of Nature, 128
Phlogiston, 24, 65
Physics, 25, 32
Pilgrim Fathers, 96
Planets, 78
Plato, 10, 11, 14, 15, 17, 20, 21–2,
    29, 30, 32, 33, 36, 84, 85, 95,
    104, 138, 139, 140, 141, 145, 171
    Laws, 15
    Republic, 12, 15, 29
    on Justice, 29–30
    on Sparta, 33
Platonists, 13
Political appraisals, 160–80
    institutions, 44
    philosophy, 9ff.
        classical, 36ff.
    terms, new definitions, 39, 40
    words, use of, 46ff.
Politics and morals, 181–93
'Polity', 46
Pope, the, 51
Popper, Professor, 82
Positive law, 98
Positivists, 12, 13, 41, 42, 136
'Power', 50, 51, 52, 56

Prejudices, political, 13
Priests, 51, 52, 187
Primitive beliefs, 21, 104
Problems, 75–9
Proletariat, dictatorship by, 133,
    134
Proofs, search for, 86
Proportional representation, 168
Prussian State, 102
Pseudo-axioms of politics, 80
Public Relations Officers, 90
Puzzles, 75–83, 160

Questions, posing of, 14
    on political philosophy, 36–7

Rationing, 67
Real essences, illusion of, 20–30
Reality, 103, 104, 105, 106
Reason, 97, 100, 173
Redefinitions, 40, 41, 105, 133
Regulations, enforcement of, 73
Relativity, Einstein's theory of, 32,
    41
Religious mysticism, 18
Representative Government, 100
Revolution of 1688, 40
Riemann, 39
Rights, 51, 56–61, 90, 91
    'real', 58, 59
'Rights of Man', 90, 94, 100
Roman Catholic Church, 49
Rousseau, Jean Jacques, 10, 32,
    33, 74, 85, 88, 90, 92, 93, 110
    Social Contract, 91
Rule of Law, 100, 107
Russia, Tsarist, 49

Scepticism, 144–7
Science, basis of, 65
Scientific method, 18
    words, 24

Sidgwick, 85
Smith, Adam, 121
Social Democrats, 117
  Fascism, 126
  revolution, in England, 118
  solidarity, 50
  'Society', 49–50, 133
Sociology, 66, 119
Socrates, 12, 29, 145
  Crito, 68
Sophists, 145
Sparta, 84
  Plato on, 33
Spatial co-ordinates, 41
Spinoza, 91
Stalin, 85, 93, 137, 142, 143
State, the, 101, 107, 108, 114, 133
  allegiance to, 107, 108
  authority of, 51, 52
  escape from, 48, 49
  in connexion with other political
    words, 50
  in relation to the Church, 10
  in relation to the individual, 11
  meaning of, 45, 46–50
State control, 10, 26, 27
States, names of, 112
Status, 51, 104
Subjectivism, 14, 100, 126, 147–60,
  160ff., 181
Switzerland, 47, 96
Symbols, in Logic, 22
  mathematical, 22, 43
  of physics, 43
  words as, 22

Technical terms, 24
Terminology, 11, 12, 19, 23, 86,
  107
The State and the Citizen, 113
Thebes, 84
Theories, of nineteenth-century
  writers, 10
  of political philosophers, 74

Theoretical foundations of politi-
  cal thinking, 14
Third Reich, 102
  Führerprinzip, 138
Thrasymachus, 12, 36, 52
Totalitarianism, 44, 102
Trade Unions, 48, 59
Truman, President, 143

Umpires, 57, 58
Unemployment, 79, 124
U.S.S.R., 10, 11, 44, 47, 86, 100,
  112, 119, 131, 137, 168, 174
U.N.O., 47
United States of America, 9, 11,
  43, 44, 69, 84, 86, 96, 112, 119,
  126, 131, 142
  Constitution of, 96, 98
  Declaration of Independence,
    36–7
  Prohibition in, 67
Universal brotherhood, 101
Universal suffrage, 100

Vatican, the, 51
Verbal confusions, 192
  definitions, 11, 15, 23, 24, 39, 40,
    41
  usage, 47
Vienna Circle, 42, 128, 136

Welfare states, 71, 86, 87, 132
Words, as symbols, 22
  history of, 24, 25
  political, 46ff.
  use of, 23, 24, 25, 26, 27, 172
Words and concepts, distinction
  between, 12
Words and their meanings, 17ff.